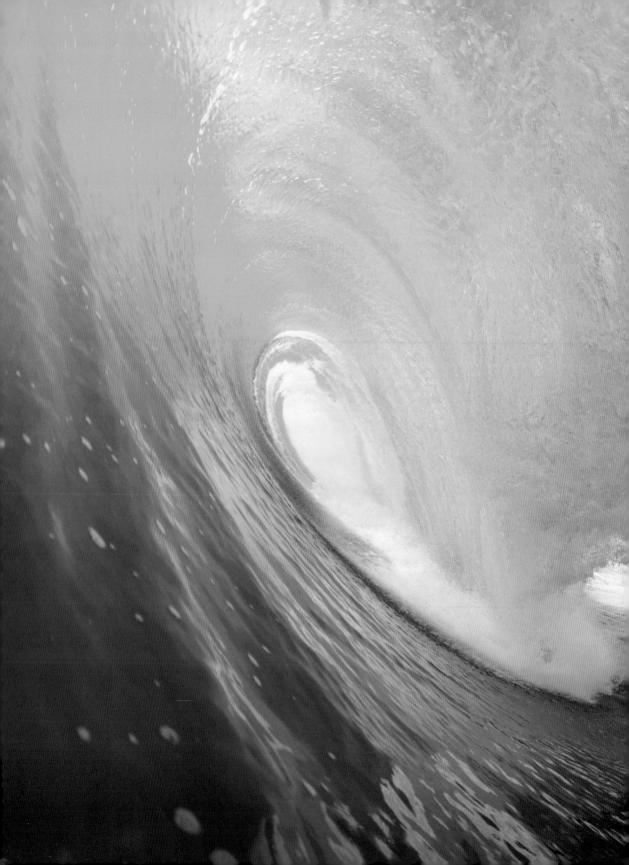

# SURFING
## SISTERHOOD
# HAWAI'I

# SURFING
# SISTERHOOD
# HAWAI'I

*Wahine Reclaiming
the Waves*

## MINDY PENNYBACKER

Mutual Publishing

page i: Rosie Jaffurs (foreground) and Leah Dawson surfing at Chuns Reef on O'ahu's North Shore. Photographer Christa Funk says, "They were sharing a wave while trying a variety of old school longboards that Randy Rarick (a pioneer Hawai'i surf event promoter) restored." Photo by Christa Funk

page iii: Surfers (Left to right) May Kamaka, Wendy Sakuma, Isabel "Izzie" Cleofe, and Mikayla Brennan posing with their surfboards before they paddle out to surf Suis (Suicides) on O'ahu. Photo by Dennis Oda

ISBN: 978-1-949307-37-5
Library of Congress Control Number: 2022950641
Cover photo by Yoshi Tanaka
Design by Jane Gillespie
First Printing, May 2023

Mutual Publishing, LLC
1215 Center Street, Suite 210
Honolulu, Hawaii 96816
Ph: (808) 732-1709
Fax: (808) 734-4094
email: info@mutualpublishing.com
www.mutualpublishing.com

Printed in South Korea

For Don, Rory and Kaitlin,
fearless chargers who keep me afloat.

Eleven-year-old Cappy Makaiau taking off on a wave at Suis (Suicides)
in front of Mākālei Beach Park on Oʻahu. Photo by Dennis Oda

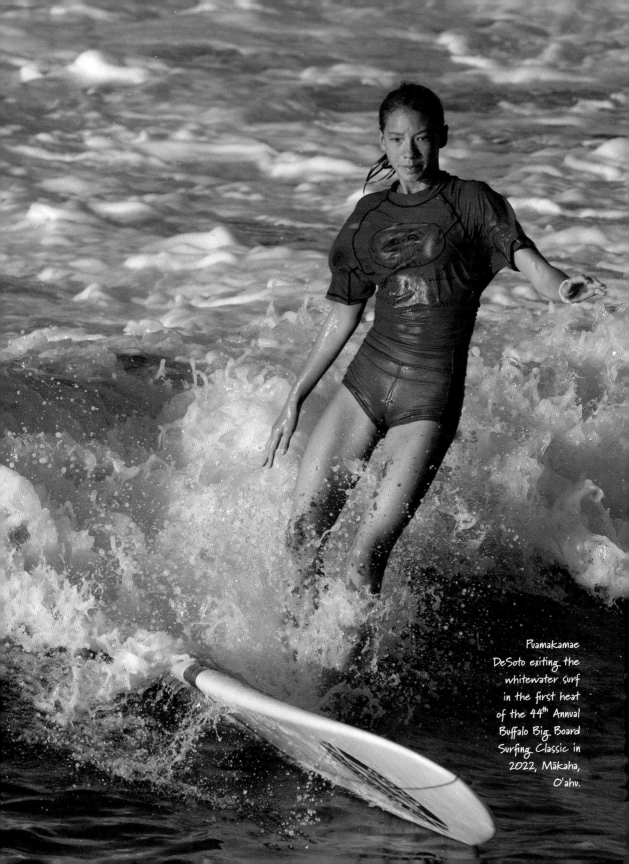

Puamakamae DeSoto exiting the whitewater surf in the first heat of the 44th Annual Buffalo Big Board Surfing Classic in 2022, Mākaha, Oʻahu.

## TABLE OF CONTENTS

INTRODUCTION ....................................... 1

WOMEN RULED THE WAVES ............... 9

WHY WE SURF ....................................25

THE SISTERS OF SUIS ....................37

MĀKAHA SISTERS............................53

TONGG'S ...........................................69

THE JOY OF SURFING......................81

TRAILBLAZERS............................. 104

OBSTACLES ...................................123

ADVICE ...........................................137

MĀLAMA HAWAI'I ........................161

TAKING FLIGHT ............................169

ENDNOTES .....................................180

BIBLIOGRAPHY .............................181

ABOUT THE COVER .......................184

PHOTO CREDITS ...........................185

ACKNOWLEDGMENTS .................189

ABOUT THE AUTHOR ...................190

Surfing at sunset.

# INTRODUCTION

Surfing is mistakenly called the sport of Hawaiian kings, leaving out the queens who equally excelled at it, and implying that only the ali'i, or aristocrats, surfed. In actuality, while the ali'i declared many prime wave sites kapu to all but their class, plenty of surf spots remained free for the maka'āinana, commoners, to enjoy. And surfing promoted social mobility, as the best surfers, male and female, were considered celebrities and highly desirable, regardless of social class.

But this much is true: Anyone feels like royalty when they're standing tall on a board on a wave.

As a maka'āinana born and raised near the Hawaiian sea, I took up surfing as a young teen and have been obsessed with it ever since. If I'd had any real athletic talent, not been so averse to cold water that I quit my Northern California college surf club, and been able to find work in Hawai'i instead of having to move to New York, I could easily have become my family's worst nightmare—a surf bum.

After all, I went surfing in a Kamehameha Day swell before my wedding and got back so late, I walked down the aisle with dripping hair. While living for decades in New York City, writing and editing for a living, I swam in city pools to stay in shape for the two weeks a year my husband, Don Wallace, our son, Rory, and I spent visiting family on O'ahu. Sometimes we'd arrive at the end of a big swell and leave just as a new one was rolling in for me to gaze upon with frustration as our airplane dipped a wing towards Diamond Head for a farewell look.

Although we lived in Lower Manhattan without a car, once in a while our uptown writer friend Bill Finnegan, the author of *Barbarian Days: A Surfing Life,* would load our boards and fins into his station wagon and drive to Long Island, where we'd tackle the dirty grey waves breaking off the rock groins of Long Beach, or the clean, turquoise cylinders rolling over the sandbars of East Hampton and Montauk. A couple times, Don and I even took the subway to the crowded Rockaways.

Benches on the Rockaways Boardwalk and view of the beach, in Queens, New York City.

I was never as obsessed with surf as Bill, who chased big, challenging waves from Fiji to Madeira. But when I met him for the first time in NYC (he and Don had been classmates and cold-water surfers at U.C. Santa Cruz), I learned we shared surfing origins. Bill had, for a time in his teens, lived in my Honolulu neighborhood and surfed the same stretch of breaks: Suis, Graveyards, Radicals, The Winch, Ricebowls, Tongg's. Although we had somehow never met at the time, he had known and surfed with my friends and mentors, the boys of the Tongg's Gang.

After more than thirty years, when I moved back to Hawai'i and into my old family home with Don, I finally got that local writing job. The *Honolulu Star-Advertiser* hired me as a reporter and ocean lifestyle columnist, a dream come true: I got to surf and write about it. The column receives steady commentary from readers, many of whom have never surfed but who simply love the ocean and are interested in the dynamics of waves and the interactions of the great diversity of

← Surfboard rentals in Waikīkī.

Women surfers
are reclaiming our
traditional wave rights
while shredding
male chauvinist myths
that we can't handle barrels
or big waves.

life forms it sustains, from coral polyps to invertebrates, fish, birds, turtles and sea mammals, including surfers.

Over the last three to four years, waves of change have rocked the surfing world, especially for Hawai'i and women athletes. Honolulu's Carissa Kainani Moore made history by winning the women's gold medal in the first-ever Olympic surfing event, held at the Tokyo Summer Games in July 2021. And in 2022, she became the first surfer and Native Hawaiian to win the AAU James E. Sullivan Award as the most outstanding U.S. college or Olympic athlete. In response to women surfers' demands for equal opportunity, the World Surf League began paying equal prize money to women and men in 2019. And following passage of a "surf equity bill" by the Honolulu City Council in 2020, the city Department of Parks and Recreation has revised its permitting rules for surf meets at O'ahu beach parks, adding gender equity as a criterion.

Women surfers, recreational as well as pro, are fast overcoming the discrimination that has impeded us since westerners invaded the islands, decimating the population with introduced disease, the illegal overthrow and annexation of their sovereign nation, impoverishment and starvation through the taking of lands and fishing rights, and suppressing the Hawaiian language and traditional practices, including

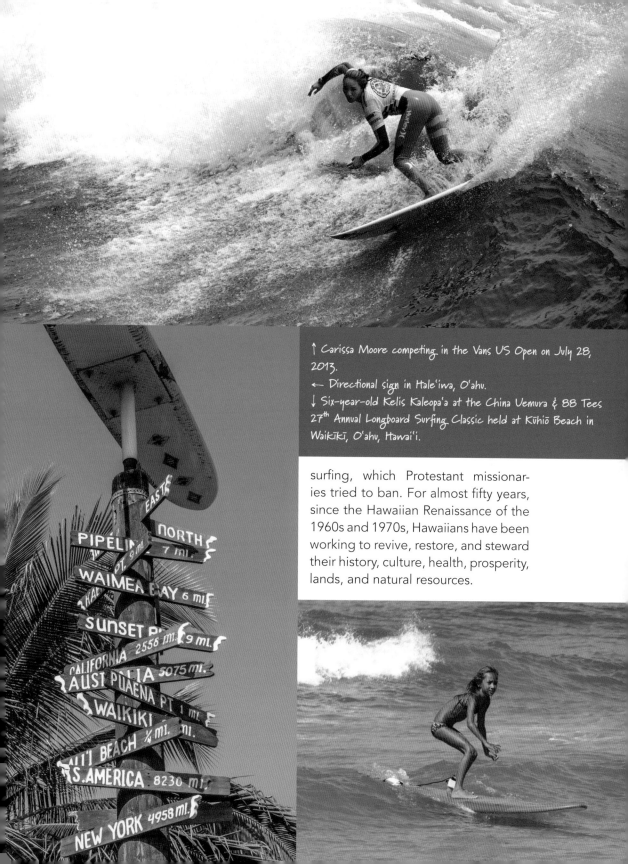

↑ Carissa Moore competing in the Vans US Open on July 28, 2013.
← Directional sign in Hale'iwa, O'ahu.
↓ Six-year-old Kelis Kaleopa'a at the China Uemura & 88 Tees 27ᵗʰ Annual Longboard Surfing Classic held at Kūhiō Beach in Waikīkī, O'ahu, Hawai'i.

surfing, which Protestant missionaries tried to ban. For almost fifty years, since the Hawaiian Renaissance of the 1960s and 1970s, Hawaiians have been working to revive, restore, and steward their history, culture, health, prosperity, lands, and natural resources.

Women surfers are reclaiming our traditional wave rights while shredding male chauvinist myths that we can't handle barrels or big waves.

Women rode Big Island tubes as early as 1836, and they have been charging through Pipeline barrels for decades. Women are riding monster waves at Pe'ahi and Waimea Bay, as well as Maverick's in Northern California and Nazaré in Portugal. Courage, skills, and drive they've got. All that has held them back is discrimination, which prevents their gaining experience and knowledge at dangerous, storied, male-packed sites like Pipeline.

"When I was a little girl, I was told that women can't surf," Hawai'i's Keala Kennelly said in an award acceptance speech in 2016, "and I was told this about getting barreled, surfing big waves, surfing Pipeline, paddling in at Jaws, and the list goes on." The award was for the Pure Scot Barrel of the Year, an open-gender category in the World Surf League's Big Wave Awards, which she was the first woman to win.

In the runup to the 2021 Tokyo Games, there were press reports of Hawaiian disappointment that Moore and Florence, a two-time world pro champion, had to wear the U.S. flag on their Olympic jerseys rather than the Hawaiian flag under which they compete on the pro circuit.

"I feel very honored to represent the U.S., but also to have represented Hawai'i in my heart the whole way through," Moore said in a phone interview after the Olympics, "and hopefully with my actions and the way I speak, people know where I'm from."

Then she described how she had felt standing on the Olympic medal stage on the beach alongside silver medalist Bianca Buitendag of South Africa and bronze winner Amuro Tsuzuki of Japan. "It was really cool to see South Africa to my right and Japan to my left, showing how the ocean connects us all, and the beautiful diversity among women who are strong all over the world," said Hawai'i's new ambassador of surfing.

Inspired by Moore's unifying vision, this book celebrates the international sisterhood of women who surf, with a focus on Hawai'i, the place where he'e nalu, wave-sliding, was born and remains an important part of indigenous culture.

↑ Local surfer Mahina Maeda on the North Shore near Sunset Beach, O'ahu. Photo by Daniel Ramirez

↑ Engraving titled "Surf-Swimming, Sandwich Islands" from *Captain Cook's Voyages Round the World*, published in 1897.

# CHAPTER 1

# WOMEN RULED THE WAVES

During the late 1960s, kids in the Tongg's Gang would hear about Hawai'i surfers who were competing on the nascent female amateur and professional circuits of the time, but we never saw their photos in magazines or films. In 1963, Californian Linda Benson was the first woman to appear on a surf magazine cover, but it didn't show Benson riding a wave. It's a portrait shot of the petite but powerful blonde, her hair in a Jean Seberg pixie cut, holding her board as she stands on land.

SURF SWIMMING, HAWAII.

As the only girl member of the gang, and a teenager learning about systemic sexism from a new wave of feminist leaders, I assumed that surfing, like most other sports and professions, had always been male-dominated. I was hopeful that, as the feminist movement gained momentum and won demands for equal opportunity, there would soon be as many women surfing as men. I was wrong.

While the number of surfers worldwide has grown exponentially to an estimated thirty-three million since the 1960s, the ratio of men to women remains unchanged, at about four to one. But on any given day the average lineup I observe in Hawaiian waves is more like eight to one, and the males regularly assert their greater strength by picking off females' rightful waves in violation of traditional surf etiquette.

Something I was surprised to learn while researching this book was that men haven't always ruled the waves. In Hawaiian history, legends, and nineteenth century newspaper accounts, women not only surfed in great numbers, but often

← Engraving titled "Surf Swimming, Hawaii" from The World's Inhabitants by G. T. Bettany, published in 1888.

dominated the scene. Although they were not allowed to eat with men and faced other gender-based restrictions under the traditional kapu system, when they got out in the ocean, Hawaiian women were free.

"The entire female population of Kealakekua plunged entirely naked into the waves" atop six- to eight-feet-long pointed boards and rode "upon the foaming crest of the surges," writes Theodore-Adolphe Barrot in his *Visit of the French Sloop of War Bonite, to the Sandwich Islands, in 1836.*[1]

"Women not only surfed, but surfed as well as men," Hawaiian waterman and historian John Clark writes in *Hawaiian Surfing: Traditions from the Past.*

Sometimes they out-surfed men. Clark cites a newspaper account of a Kamehameha Day surf contest off Lahaina, Maui, on June 11, 1887, in which a man named Poepoe was favored to win. His wife Nakookoo also competed. As her husband rides a wave, Nakookoo "shoots like a flying fish through the whitening foam, jostles the champion on his wonted plank of victory, and came in foremost amid the outcries of a delighted multitude glad that the woman had won." The writer added that Nakookoo, while still beautiful, was not in her first youth, so it's also a win against ageism.

Clark, who conducts extensive primary research in nineteenth century Hawaiian-language and English-language newspapers, said, "As far as I know, this is the first description in English of a surfing contest, and it was won by a woman."

Clark points out that women also got covered up, or tubed, as Barrot observed. As they rode a

"THE ENTIRE FEMALE POPULATION OF KEALAKEKUA PLUNGED ENTIRELY NAKED INTO THE WAVES" ATOP SIX- TO EIGHT-FEET-LONG POINTED BOARDS AND RODE "UPON THE FOAMING CREST OF THE SURGES."

↑ Watercolor titled "Bathing Scene, Lahaina, Maui" by James Gay Sawkins, 1855.

wave, the Frenchman wrote, "the least movement of their body gave to the plank the desired direction, and disappearing for a moment in the midst of the breakers, they very soon arose from the foam."[2]

Although Barrot did not have a word for barrel or tube, this passage, Clark says, clearly describes the surfers entering the barrel, vanishing entirely from sight behind the whitewater curtain and then finding the exit to reappear, spit out with a ball of foam.

Clark calls this "the earliest description by a westerner of tube-riding, the radical maneuver that is commonly assumed to be a 20th-century invention."

Many of the most famous surfers in Hawaiian legend and history were female, starting with the volcano goddess Pele and her sister Hiʻiaka, goddess of the hula, the traditional dance closely linked to surfing. Many Hawaiʻi women today practice both.

"We know from moʻolelo (stories) and history that Hawaiian women surfed," says Hawaiian cultural adviser Uʻilani Macabio, who dances hula and surfs. "I grew up hearing stories about Queen Ka'ahumanu (wife of King Kamehameha I) surfing Maliu, or Lighthouse, in Kohala (Big Island)—that's sometimes a heavy wave...and on a skegless board!"

Ka'ahumanu was the daughter of another famous woman surfer, the Maui chiefess Nāmāhana, who was "reckoned one of the most expert at that diversion," according Peter Puget, a lieutenant who sailed aboard the *Discovery* under George Vancouver from 1791-1795.[3]

Puget recounts walking in 1794 with Nāmāhana and her husband, Big Island chief Ke'eaumoku, to "a small stony beach where the natives were amusing themselves in the surf on swimming boards."[4]

There, Nāmāhana "immediately (stripped) naked and she certainly notwithstanding her corpulency performed her part with wonderful dexterity," Puget writes. "The first sea or surf that brought her in to the beach was immensely high, (and) on its top she came, floating on a broad board till the break[er] had nearly reached the rocks; she then suddenly turned."[5]

← A depiction of Chief Kalanimoku and his wife, Likelike, with a long surfboard (olo) in foreground by artist Alphonse Pellion, circa 1819. Bishop Museum

→ Native Hawaiian surfer circa 1890s, photo by Theodore P. Severin. Hawai'i State Archives

A high level of skill was required to ride a traditional Hawaiian surfboard, known as an olo, kīko'o or alaia, depending on its length and shape, cut and custom-shaped for its rider from the trunk of an 'ulu (breadfruit), wiliwili (native balsa), or koa (native hardwood) tree. The board's smooth bottom gave it speed but made it far more challenging to maneuver than modern foam-and-fiberglass boards affixed with a skeg that, like a boat's rudder, provides stability and makes it easy to turn.

# Descriptions of Queen Kaʻahumanu and King Kamehameha I riding waves

feature in *Fragments of Hawaiian History* by John (Ioane) Papa Īʻī, the seminal Hawaiian historian, educator and political leader who was born in 1800 and served in the royal court. The practice of surfing by both sexes is illustrated in an anecdote about Īʻī's mother, Kalaikane Wanaoʻa Pahulemu. "Her family fondly called her Pahulemu, or shoved from behind, for her poor surfing skills. (She was unable to catch a wave unless someone started her off with a push)," Marie Alohalani Brown writes in her biography, *Facing the Spears of Change: The Life and Legacy of John Papa ʻĪʻi.*[28]

At a gnarly spot called Koʻokā, in Puaa, North Kona, where surf broke over a coral head lying off a lava-rock point, the royal couple paddled out to the break in a canoe, carrying their surfboards, with which they "leaped out of the canoe and rode the crest of the wave ashore," Īʻī writes. The practice was known as lele waʻa: "This art was held in esteem at that time, and so the surfing places were constantly filled with men and women."

Koʻokā was perilous with the rocks, between which the surfer had to ride. "This was a difficult feat and one not often seen, but for Kaahumanu and the king it was easy," Īʻī writes. "When they reached the place where the surf rose high, they went along with the crest of a wave and slipped into the sea pool before the wave rolled over. The spectators shouted and remarked to each other how clever the two were."

Īʻī also describes how Kaʻahumanu surfed with

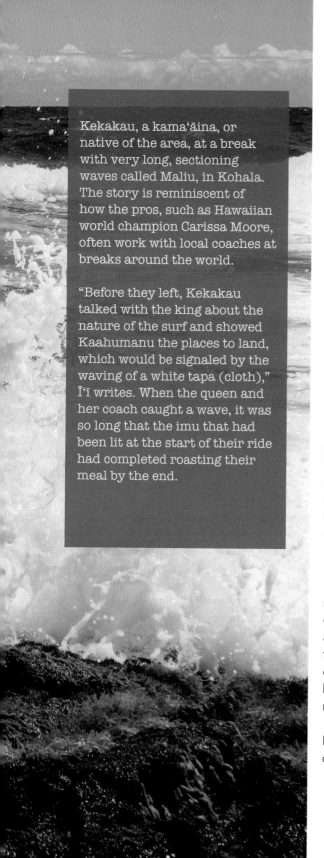

Kekakau, a kama'āina, or native of the area, at a break with very long, sectioning waves called Maliu, in Kohala. The story is reminiscent of how the pros, such as Hawaiian world champion Carissa Moore, often work with local coaches at breaks around the world.

"Before they left, Kekakau talked with the king about the nature of the surf and showed Kaahumanu the places to land, which would be signaled by the waving of a white tapa (cloth)," Ī'ī writes. When the queen and her coach caught a wave, it was so long that the imu that had been lit at the start of their ride had completed roasting their meal by the end.

Legends from the millennium before western contact tell happier stories about women wave riders. The most famous of these heroines is Kelea, who loved surfing more than anything.

"My favorite story is of Kelea the surfing princess goddess from Maui, the best ocean woman ever, and a trickster too," said U'ilani Macabio. "She has this wit and cunning and fast mouth, really smart."

A sister of the mō'ī, or ruling chief, of Maui island and a chiefess in her own right, Kelea lived near the sea at Hāna "because of the surf riding there, reveling in the curling breakers of the midmorning when the sea was smooth and even,"[6] writes Samuel Mānaiakalani Kamakau, the Hawaiian scholar who was the first to record many legends, including the story of Kelea, which he set down in 1865.

"Surfing was her greatest pleasure," Kamakau writes. "She enjoyed surfing so much that at night she dwelt upon the morrow's surfing and awakened to the murmuring of the sea to take up her board. The early morning, too, was delightful because of its coolness, and so she might go at dawn."[7]

I found it thrilling and somehow endorsing to read that this heroine of

dismissed her brother's "reform cabinet" and rewrote the constitution. She also wrote many songs, most famously "Aloha 'Oe" and "Ke Aloha O Ka Haku/ The Queen's Prayer," which I remember singing after "America the Beautiful" and "The Pledge of Allegiance" every morning at Jefferson Elementary School.

'O Kamaka'eha ka honua nalu
A pae o Kamaka'eha i ka nalu.
Kamaka'eha on the crest
Rides the surf to shore.

Using one of her many given names, Lili'uokalani's surfing mele celebrates how "Kamaka'eha on the crest/ Rides the surf to shore." Clark notes a parallel meaning of the Hawaiian words in the chant describe the queen as both the foundation and top of the state, providing guidance and stability. She only reigned for three years, however, before her government was illegally overthrown at gunpoint by the Americans in 1893.

The surfbreak Queen's in Waikīkī is named for Lili'uokalani, who had a beach house there.

# Surfing mele, or chants, were dedicated to Hawaiian royalty,

including the Kingdom of Hawai'i's last monarch, Queen Lili'uokalani, who was born Lydia Lili'u Lōloku Walania Wewehi Kamaka'eha in 1838. She fought to restore the integrity of the constitutional monarchy after American residents in the kingdom forced her late brother, King Kalākaua, to sign a "bayonet constitution" that prevented Native Hawaiians from voting and placed his government under their control. Lili'uokalani

↑ King Kalākaua and others on beach with what is belieaved to be the oldest photograph of a Hawaiian surfer in the background, circa 1887. Hawai'i State Archives

old Hawai'i preferred glassy, windless conditions and did the occasional dawn patrol session, just like me. These details humanized and enlivened the past with a sense that Hawai'i's people and waves haven't changed much, despite all the upheavals and loss they have suffered. Reading Kamakau, I could imagine that Kelea and I might one day find ourselves riding the same wave through time. The story and the way Kamakau wrote it confirmed my long-held feeling that riding a wave serves up a slice of eternity.

In search of a wife, an O'ahu chief named Lo-Lale, of Līhu'e, an inland district on that island, sent a wa'a ka 'ili wahine, or wife-snatching canoe, to visit the neighbor islands and find him a woman. Hearing of Kelea's beauty and passion for wave rid-ing, the crew sailed to Hāna, invited her to join them for a canoe surf, and kidnapped her to O'ahu.

↑ This engraving by Wallis Mackay illustrates Hawaiian women riding surf-boards while others dive under the waves in Charles Warren Stoddard's "Summer Cruising in the South Seas", 1874, Chatto and Windus, London. Bishop Museum

There in the Līhu'e highlands, she lived for ten years as Lo-Lale's wife, bearing him three children and never once getting down to the ocean. Finally, she asked his permission to go sightseeing at the nearest seashore, in 'Ewa. He agreed, acknowledging that for Kelea, "living on our inland land is dejecting,"[8] and doubtless guessing he'd never see her again.

His guess was correct. As Kelea and her guides traveled east across the 'Ewa plain, she heard of a place where the chiefs enjoyed surfing and "desire rose in her."[9] She asked her companions to take her to that place, which was Waikīkī, and when they arrived and saw the chiefs surfing, Kelea asked if someone would lend her a board, "and perhaps because she was so beautiful a woman, someone gave her one."[10]

Like a pilgrim entering a sacred place, she rubbed the red dirt of 'Ewa from her feet at the water's edge before she entered the sea, dipped herself in it before getting on the board, and paddled out to the break where she sat a courteous space apart from the local surfers and waited for the fourth wave. While riding, "she showed herself unsurpassed in skill and grace"[11] so that all the people "burst out in cheering."[12]

The surfing ali'i nui of Waikīkī, the high chief Kalamakua, who had heard the stories of Kelea's wave riding fame, ran down to the water's edge to greet her, took her off to his kapu place, and they were married.

Kelea's surfing is a proud part of the heritage all daughters of the islands share. She's an inspiration to us all, that inner voice who sets us free from the nagging ties of duty to fling care to the winds and just go for it when the surf is good.

Another legendary Hawaiian surfer was Māmala, the namesake of the Sea of Māmala, the great bay whose turquoise waters stretch from Diamond Head through Waikīkī to Honolulu Harbor.

"Mamala was a chiefess of Kupua character,"[13] writes William Westervelt, a former missionary who became a researcher in Hawaiian language, history and mythology, in his "A Surfing Legend," in 1913.

"This meant that she was a mo'o or gigantic lizard or crocodile, as well as a beautiful woman, and could assume whichever shape she most desired,"[14] and in her human form, "Mamala was a wonderful surf rider,"[15] Westervelt writes. "Very skillfully she danced on the roughest waves. The surf in which she most delighted rose far out in the rough sea, where the winds blew strong and white-caps were on waves which rolled in rough disorder into the bay of Kou [Honolulu]."[16]

Her performances drew appreciative public audiences. "The people on the beach, watching her, filled the air with resounding applause as they clapped their hands over her extraordinary athletic feats."[17]

But as with Kelea, Māmala was desired for her beauty and wave riding prowess, and romantic complications arose. Originally married to the shark-man Ouha, with whom she enjoyed gambling with kōnane (a board game like checkers, played with pebbles on a smooth stone), Māmala was forced to leave him to become the wife of the chief Honoka'upu. Westervelt includes a lovely mele, or chant, in which

# Queen Lili'uokalani's niece and heir to the throne,

Princess Victoria Kawēkiu Lunalilo Kalaninuiahilapalapa Ka'iulani Cleghorn, traveled to Washington, D.C. with her aunt and met with President Grover Cleveland, petitioning but ultimately unable to prevent the illegal annexation of Hawai'i by the U.S. in 1898.

Raised in Waikīkī by her parents, Princess Likelike and Archibald Cleghorn, at their estate 'Āinahau, Ka'iulani loved to swim and surf; one of her surfboards, a thin, slender alaia model made of koa, seven-foot, four-inches long, is in the collection of the Bishop Museum in Honolulu.

The princess also loved to surf in outrigger canoe, and in June 1898, following an honorary luncheon on the beach, the travel writer Burton Holmes, author of the eponymous "Travelogues," found himself riding waves with Ka'iulani in a canoe surf session off Waikīkī. While a complete newcomer, he recognized the skill and strength the practice required as everyone paddled hard to reach "a speed that permits the towering wall of water to overtake the canoe and lift up the stern." As the boat raced shoreward at thirty miles per hour, Holmes wrote, "There before me is the Princess Kaiulani, her faced aglow with excitement, shouting and paddling frantically, her eyes flashing with the wild pleasure of it all."

Less than a year and a half later, in March 1899, Ka'iulani fell ill after being caught in a rainstorm while riding horseback in the mountains of the Big Island and died at age twenty-four.

In modern times, Kalehuawehe, now known as Castles, was the break where Duke Kahanamoku began his legendary ride, taking off on an enormous "cloudbreak" wave twenty-five feet high, and steering and trimming his skegless hardwood board westward through consecutive breaks for more than a mile, before finally riding to shore at Canoes at Waikīkī.

Māmala speaks of her "dear husband Ouha,"[18] who she misses, while acknowledging, at the same time, "I belong to Honokaupu/From the top of the tossing surf waves."[19]

Romance was a prevailing theme in Hawaiian surfing tales, which Westervelt deemed "the most interesting" of all Hawaiian legends. They portray women and men falling in love while riding waves together, and men and women vying for the attentions of the opposite sex.

One of the many kanikau, or lamentations, written for Princess Ka'iulani evokes Kalehuawehe, "the most famous surf spot in Waikiki," Clark writes, which "was also well known among Hawaiians as a poetic symbol of great loss."[20]

A romantic interlude between surfers gave Kalehuawehe its name, which means "the lehua flower lei removed," according to Clark. In Kamakau's version of the legend, Pikoiaka'alala, a "strikingly handsome"[21] warrior, was surfing at an unnamed break where commoners were permitted when he was joined by Kahamalu'ihi, a Waikīkī chiefess, who had left the nearby kapu surf spot of Kapua, reserved for ali'i like herself, and followed him.

Pikoiaka'alala was wearing lehua flower lei as he sat in the lineup preening "with a grin and a coy look."[22]

Kicking off a flirty conversation layered with kaona, the hidden mean-

↑ Duke Kahanamoku statue in Waikīkī.

ings Hawaiians weave through stories and songs, Kahamalu'ihi said, "I think I'd look fine with your lei."[23]

The warrior replied, "my lei are free for all,"[24] implying, Kamakau says, that since he was a commoner and she was an ali'i, his lei wouldn't be good enough for her.

Kahamalu'ihi replied that once she wore a lei or surfed a board, it ceased to be available to anyone and "belongs to me only,"[25] therefore it would be good enough for her.

Playing dumb, Pikoiaka'alala teased, "What lei are you talking about?"[26] although, Kamakau notes he "understood what the chiefess was talking about."[27] The warrior then removed his lei, tying them around her neck, and from then on the break was known as Kalehuawehe.

I love this story in particular because it shows how surfing provided an escape from the kapu system that strictly regulated social interactions onshore. Then, as now, people of diverse backgrounds intermingled at non-kapu breaks where status was awarded by skill rather than breeding.

Lehua lei are popular metaphors for surfer love in many mo'olelo and mele. In Martha Beckwith's *Romances*, Lā'ieikawai, the princess of Paliuli, throws a lehua lei around the neck of the surfer Haua'iliki after he skillfully rides a wave she directed him to take.

But wearing another woman's lei could be considered cheating. In Beckwith's *The Legend of Kawelo*, a wife decked her husband in lehua lei every morning before he surfed Paumalū, the big-wave break of Sunset Beach on O'ahu's North Shore. One day, a woman on the beach placed 'ilima lei around his neck; from afar, his wife saw the rival lei and asked her ancestral gods to punish him. As he climbed the hill homeward, his body felt heavy and as turned back for a last glimpse of the waves, the gods turned him to stone.

As all surfers who have been sidelined by injury know, few things can feel worse than being stuck on shore when the waves are good. Poor Kawelo was doomed to stare helplessly at his favorite surf spot for eternity. When I read his legend, I recognized one of my recurrent nightmares in which the surf is up and I am walking to the water with my board, but my legs grow heavier and heavier until I'm stuck, immobilized, in the sand.

In traditional Hawaiian culture, established couples also surfed together, from Ka'ahumanu and Kamehameha to Nakookoo and Poepoe. However, it's rare to see romantic partners surfing together today. Over the years, I can think of only a handful of couples—Nicole Irie and Marc Lambert, Genevieve and Mark Sullivan, and Courtney and Greg Gussmann—who've come out to Suis and were obviously enjoying each other's company, flirting, and joking around. By now, some have children, which makes it harder to surf together. They take turns babysitting and surfing.

Moms will carve out time to surf, even if conditions aren't ideal, because they need the freedom, refreshment, and renewal getting out in the ocean provides. They'll seize the moment on their own, or, in a recent trend, meet in organized groups such as Surfing Moms, whose members take turns watching everyone's kids on the beach while the others surf.

And young women and girls are organizing, too, gathering together for activities and support in groups such as Carissa Moore's Moore Aloha, a nonprofit organization founded in 2018 by the young Hawaiian world surfing champion and her family, including sister Cayla Moore. Its mission, as stated on its website moorealoha.com, "is to empower young women to be strong, confident and compassionate individuals" using surfing as a platform.

Moore Aloha's goal is to hold three to four events a year for sixty to eighty girls and women. Partnering with other community nonprofits and "using our combined girl power at each event," the organization aims to "continue a ripple effect of love and aloha in our communities," as the girls share and practice the surfing, healthy living, positive self-imaging and communication skills they've learned.

Look at the smiles of the girls pictured on moorealoha.com and the excitement and pride on the face of any young surfer on a wave, and you understand the perfect affirmation of Moore's vision: Girl power is here.

IN TRADITIONAL HAWAIIAN CULTURE,
ESTABLISHED COUPLES ALSO SURFED TOGETHER,
FROM KA'AHUMANU AND KAMEHAMEHA
TO NAKOOKOO AND POEPOE.

↑ Surf Riding in Waikīkī. Hawai'i State Archives

# CHAPTER 2

# WHY
# WE SURF

Most local girls started out in the same, informal way. The kai, the ocean, is the first playground for Hawai'i's children; they frolic endlessly in the shallows, splashing and diving and laughing, washing up and down the beach in gentle shore break. They learn about the movements of wind and water and to be relaxed but vigilant in the kai before gradually, over the years, venturing farther out to try bodysurfing or riding a board.

← Local surfer Mahina Maeda on the North Shore near Sunset Beach, O'ahu. Photo by Daniel Ramirez

"We were all little girls, always going to the beach, playing around while my father fished, and then we started using boards, working with the waves," remembered U'ilani Macabio, a history teacher and Hawaiian cultural adviser on the Big Island of Hawai'i. "I started surfing at Pohoiki First Bay in sixth grade. Pretty much we'd just go, learn on our own, a sink or swim sorta deal. You had to watch out—if you didn't pay attention, the current would push you and you wouldn't realize until it was too late, and you'd end up on the rocks with wana (spiny sea urchins) all over your body," she added with a laugh. Why does she surf?

"The fun thing about surfing," U'ilani said, "is it is truly the Hawaiian rollercoaster ride. It's, like, addicting."

That rollercoaster has lately been riding higher and faster, like a surfer accelerating to take flight off the top of the wave and perform an aerial spin. A major impetus was surfing's long-awaited debut as an Olympic event, where the high level of surfing in extreme conditions at Japan's Tsurigasaki Beach galvanized a worldwide television audience. Moore won by finding enough shape and space in the big, chaotic typhoon waves to carve her signature power turns, deep cutbacks and rhythmic, flowing lines.

Less than two months later, after turning twenty-nine in August, Moore showed her resilience and grit by battling for and gaining her fifth world title in a new, winner-takes-all format at Lower Trestles, California.

Carrying forward the century-old legacy of Duke Paoa Kahanamoku, the Olympic swimming gold medalist and Hawai'i's ambassador of surfing and aloha, Moore's many victories and her genuine aloha spirit have reestablished the islands' supremacy in the surfing world.

↑ Cappy Makaiau paddling in at Mākālei Beach, O'ahu. Photo by Dennis Oda

To surfers, the old island saying "lucky you live Hawai'i" ought to be "lucky you surf Hawai'i." The islands enjoy warm water and waves year-round and house more storied, coveted breaks than any other place on earth: Waikīkī, Ala Moana Bowls, Mākaha, Hale'iwa, Waimea Bay, Banzai Pipeline, Sunset Beach, Hanalei Bay, Honolua Bay and Pe'ahi ("Jaws"). It is a deeply held conviction among surfers worldwide that the big, hollow, lethally powerful waves of O'ahu's North Shore are the ultimate rite of passage and proving ground.

It's been that way since the mid-twentieth century, when Greg Noll, Harry Scurch, Mickey Munoz, Fred Van Dyke, George Downing, and Peter Cole first surfed the giant waves of Waimea Bay. But Hawaiians were there first, Karin Amimoto Ingersoll says in her book on surfing, *Waves of Knowing: a Seascape Epistemology.* "Kanaka Maoli (Native Hawaiians) undeniably rode and named the waves at Waimea Bay and elsewhere," Ingersoll writes, citing a kau, or sacred chant, from a mo'olelo (story) of Hi'iaka, the surfing goddess of hula. There are also mo'olelo about surfing at Paumalū, which westerners later renamed Sunset Beach.

With a population of only 1.4 million, Hawai'i has a disproportionately high profile in competitive surfing. Among the eighteen women who qualified for the 2022 World Surf League champi-

→ *Carissa Moore winning the 2019 Women's Pro Championship at the 2019 Lululemon Maui Pro Surf Competition.*

Carissa Moore was the only one on the four-member U.S. team to receive a medal for surfing in the 2020 Summer Olympics; the women's silver medal went to South Africa's Bianca Buitendag, and Japan's Amuro Tsuzuki took bronze; Florida native Caroline Marks placed fourth for the U.S. On the men's side, the affable, airborne Italo Ferreira won gold for Brazil, California native Kanoa Igarashi took silver for Japan, and Australia's Owen Wright earned bronze. Also surfing for the U.S., Californian Kolohe Andino finished in fourth place, and Hawai'i's John John Florence placed ninth.

After paddling in from her victory heat and being chaired up the beach on the shoulders of the U.S. team coaches, beaming a wide smile, her right hand raised high in the Hawaiian "shaka" sign, Moore thanked and praised her teammates, who had cheered her from the desolate beach dotted with socially distanced spectators. The four U.S. Olympians had roomed together in a Covid "bubble," keeping each others' spirits up while separated from their partners and families.

↑ Going surfing at Waikīkī Beach.
Photo by Prayitno

onship tour, five came from Hawai'i, five from Australia (population 25 million), three from California (39 million), and one each from Florida (21 million), France (67 million), Costa Rica (5 million) and Brazil (212 million). And the Costa Rican and Brazilian surfers were raised in Hawai'i.

Olympic surfing, to be held next in the mediagenic, room-size blue barrels of Teahupo'o, Tahiti, during the 2024 Paris Summer Games, is predicted to stimulate more growth in the already booming sport. There are an estimated 35 million practitioners worldwide, according to a 2016 report by the International Surfing Association.

The ISA added that eighty percent of surfers worldwide are male, a four to one ratio that correlates with what I see in the lineup every day.

A neighbor and regular observer of our local beach scene says when men paddle out they look serious, even grim, as if psyching themselves up for battle. Whereas women, he said, look happy and lighthearted,

as if they're going out to play. He adds he sees more women paddling out alone, whereas men go out in posses of bros, or brahs.

Why the difference? A woman's life, like surfing, is a balancing act. We tend to go out alone because there are fewer of us who surf and we have less time. With everyone's different obligations and schedules, it's hard to schedule meetups with friends. We have to seize the moment when we can, often on the spur of the moment, grabbing a quick break from child care, elder care, pet care, errands or homemaking duties, or before or after telecommuting, or working outside our homes.

A WOMAN'S LIFE, LIKE SURFING, IS A BALANCING ACT.

↑ Practicing yoga on a SUP at Ala Moana State Park, O'ahu.

Karin Amimoto Ingersoll, a mother of two who used to go to sleep every night and wake up every morning thinking of surf, said she hasn't surfed in years. "When I get in the ocean, I'm boogie boarding with my kids," she said.

Recently, however, women are finding companionship and time in organized groups like the nonprofit, Surfing Moms, whose members take turns watching everyone's kids on the beach while others surf.

↑ Amelia Borofsky, a member of Surfing Moms O'ahu, hugs her child during a moms-and-kids meetup on Waikīkī Beach. Photo by Candace Stalder, Surfing Moms

Surfing provides "a bit of meditation, takes me out of my zone of worry, all the things, schedules, that come with everyday life—I've got to focus on waves, that's it," said Surfing Moms founder Elizabeth Madin, a mother of three and marine biologist whose husband, Josh Madin, is also a marine biologist. "I'm just glad to be out there, doesn't matter if I get the best wave."

She modelled Surfing Moms after Surfing Mums, a group she joined when the couple was living in Australia. "Until I found Surfing Mums, I took a hiatus of four to five years from surfing because it was just too hard," she said.

When the family moved to O'ahu, where Elizabeth and Josh are faculty members at the Hawai'i Institute of Marine Biology, she started a Surfing Moms in Kailua, where they live, and has since added chapters in Honolulu, 'Ewa Beach, and Lahaina, Maui. In addition to getting moms back in the water, the group helps build community, Elizabeth said. She has become close friends with women she might not otherwise have met and meets other surfers through them, expanding her network so that she often recognizes friendly faces whenever and wherever she goes out. "When I'm out there with friends I'm not as intimidated," she said. "When I'm alone, I feel I have to be expressionless, keep to myself."

Women's attitudes towards surfing evolve as our responsibilities grow: we're less picky about waves and conditions than we used to be. When we see an opening, we just grab the moment and go.

"I think it's changed for me throughout the years," said Sally Lundburg, a Big Island filmmaker, farmer and high school teacher. "Now, just being busy, a mom and a teacher, I'll take any time I can get in ocean, whether swimming, bodysurfing, surfing, it really doesn't matter the conditions just to reconnect with my body and nature. I can feel renewed by going out on the worst days."

"Surfing feels liberating, like, oh, I've been holding my breath for so long and all of a sudden I get to release it," U'ilani Macabio, a working mother of two, says in a 2018 video made by Sally Lundburg at Waipi'o Valley, where they both surfed regularly with friends and family until the county's sudden closure of the only beach

↑ Surfing Moms members take turns babysitting the children on Kailua Beach while other members paddle out for a surf sesh. Photo by KC Lostetter Photography, Surfing Moms

access road in February 2022. Their community continues to struggle to restore and protect public access to the ocean at Waipi'o.

Most of the girls and women who share their stories in these pages began surfing out of love for the ocean, but a few were motivated to face and conquer their fear of waves and the sea.

Some were born and raised in the islands, while others have moved here, fallen in love with surfing (and sometimes a local resident), and stayed.

For many women, surfing is a way to perpetuate traditional Hawaiian values and restore one's sense of self. Ingersoll writes, "It isn't until I enter ke kai (the sea) for he'e nalu that I am able to connect with my Kanaka (Hawaiian) heritage."

For others, it's a way to bond with loved ones. Many were taught by their fathers, some by their mothers. But not everyone is born into a surfing family, so several learned in formal lessons or simply by paddling out with a group of friends.

And there are so many more reasons. If you don't surf, you can try it and add your own.

But watch out: The first time you stand up on a board, borne swiftly along by a wave, you could become obsessed.

↑← Kristi Hallock kisses her child before paddling out, while other Surfing Moms members watch the children on Kailua Beach, O'ahu.
→ Left to right: Alyssa Myers, Anna Shoemaker, Elizabeth Madin, and Uliana Box, members of Surfing Moms, pose with their surfboards and children on Kailua Beach. All photos by KC Lostetter Photography, Surfing Moms

URFING FEELS LIBERATING, LIKE, OH,
VE BEEN HOLDING MY BREATH FOR
O LONG AND ALL OF A SUDDEN I GET
O RELEASE IT. — U'ILANI MACABIO

# All you need to join in is a love for the ocean

and to try and get in it as much as you can. The dense salt water buoys you up and washes off tensions. Float on your back and watch the clouds. Dive through crystal waves or bob in whitewater. In such moments, women can feel not only liberated, but truly free. After swimming in a clear ocean at low tide on an offshore wind, you don't need to shower; you've been rinsed clean.

No matter how little time I have before a flight, I never leave the islands without racing down to the beach, taking a quick plunge in the sea, and leaving the salt water in my hair and on my skin as I dry off and pull on my traveling clothes. I'm always the last out the door, which is why we usually get a text from the cat sitter asking, did we mean to leave the front door open when we left?

When I come home, the first thing I do, after setting down my bags and petting the cat, is pull on my swimsuit and rush down to the seashore to dive in, wash off the grime and stress of the journey, and check the waves.

↑ The author surfing Suis. Photos copyright
© 2022 by E.Y.Y. Yanagi

Veteran surfers (left to right) Evelyn Black, author Mindy Pennybacker, Kai'ulu Downing, Kim Heyer, and Melissa Kurpinski pose with their surfboards at Mākālei Beach Park after a morning surf session at Suis. Photo by Dennis Oda

# CHAPTER 3

# THE SISTERS OF SUIS

As a Honolulu surfer who hates to search for parking, I seldom paddle out anywhere but directly offshore of my neighborhood by the sea. My regular surf spot is Suis, a shifty, challenging, often maddening break that lies off the western point of Lēʻahi, Diamond Head Crater.

Suis is short for Suicides, the original name, which derives from the menacing aspect of the barrier reef, with its toothy coral heads you have to thread through to reach the waves. When asked how the spot got the name, we neighborhood kids used to reply, "because it's suicide to go there," in the hopes of discouraging people from trying and crowding up what we considered our private break.

→ Melissa Kurpinski surfs a wave at Suis. Photo by Dennis Oda

THERE'S A RUMOR THAT SOMEBODY HAD ACTUALLY DONE AWAY WITH HIMSELF AT SUICIDES, MAYBE BACK IN THE 1950S, BUT IT'S NEVER BEEN SUBSTANTIAT- ED. ACCIDENTAL DROWN- INGS HAVE OCCURRED THERE, AS WELL AS AT LEAST ONE FATAL STROKE AND CRITICAL INJURIES CAUSED BY COLLISIONS WITH SURFBOARDS OR THE REEF, EVEN ON SMALL DAYS. A FIERCE PREVAILING WIND CHURNS THE STEEP, FAST WAVES, AND IF YOU FALL OFF YOUR BOARD AT LOW TIDE YOU CAN HIT YOUR HEAD ON THE SHALLOW REEF, AS I HAVE LEARNED FIRSTHAND.

As the crow flies, Suis breaks about 200 yards offshore from a narrow sliver of beach. I used to be able to look out my bed-room window to check the Suicides lineup, the place in the water where the waves rise up and form. Now several mega-mansions block the view, so along with most of the world, I have to walk down to the beach for a surf check.

One Saturday in March, I walked down to the shore to see crisp, fun-size waves, shoulder- to head-high, peeling left and right along the reef. I rushed home, put on my spring wetsuit, waxed my board, grabbed my helmet, and rushed back to the beach, leaving my rubber slippers at the top of the steps leading down to the sand, which resembles the footwear-strewn front porch of a local home or Buddhist shrine.

I paddled out to find seven guys and one woman, my neighbor Andree Paradis, in the lineup. Now there were two women. For as long as I can remember, girls have been outnumbered in the surf by boys.

38

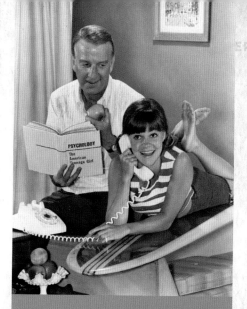

# When I started surfing in 1966,

I was motivated by the music of the Beach Boys; the *Gidget* TV show starring Sally Field, from the novel about a girl who infiltrates an all-boy surf gang; and the all-boy surf group in my neighborhood known as the Tongg's Gang.

That year also saw the release of the seminal surf documentary and travelogue, *The Endless Summer,* by Californian Bruce Browne. As a brown-skinned, mixed-race girl, I was disappointed by the film's white-male cast and their condescension toward Africans, Latin Americans, and Polynesians. I knew how it felt to be on the other end of that

↑ Actor Don Porter as Russell Lawrence and actress Sally Field as his teenage daughter, Gidget, on the TV show Gidget.

gaze, having been informed, by a pale-skinned tourist who tried to chat me up in the surf, how amazing it was that I spoke such perfect English.

Regardless, the film was a hit, earning $20 million in box office receipts worldwide and stoking a craze for the freewheeling, surfing lifestyle it portrayed. In the 60s, participation in the sport grew "from a few hundred post-war surfers (to an estimated) 40,000 in California alone," according to *Surfer Today* magazine.

By 2016, there were thirty-five million surfers worldwide, the International Surfing Association (ISA) estimated in a report it gave to the International Olympic Committee as part of its pitch for surfing to become an Olympic sport.

"BUOYANT FUN... HYPNOTIC BEAUTY AND CONTINUOUS EXCITEMENT."
—N.Y. Times

"MAGNIFICENT FILM. NOT TO BE MISSED."
—Harper's Bazaar

# The Endless Summer

IN COLOR

Produced, directed, edited by Bruce Brown • Featuring: Mike Hynson • Robert August • Distributed by Cinema V

↑ Lobby card for the 1966 movie The Endless Summer.

As I paddled out to Suis that Saturday in early spring, I saw Andree hop on a wave a guy had tried for but missed. Standing tall on her longboard, she rode it all the way in, gliding down the line and carving gentle turns in her classic, casual stance, back and long legs straight, long, straight hair flowing past her shoulders. I gave an approving hoot as she passed by.

"Hey, where's your longboard?" Andree asked me as she paddled back out. She likes to point out I'd catch a lot more waves with a bigger board, which floats better and paddles faster. But I'm too lazy to carry a heavy longboard for three blocks.

As I found my favorite takeoff spot by triangulating my landmarks—a chimney, two trees, the lighthouse against Lē'ahi's slope—the guys, all strangers, pretended they didn't notice me. This was also typical. While some guys smile and say hi, most act as if I'm beneath notice, dismissing me as one of the weaker surfers of

First-time Suis surfer Mikayla Brennan (far right) is all smiles as she watches veteran surfer Kim Heyer (blue cap) catch a wave. Photo by Dennis Oda

the weaker sex, and old, to boot. Surfing, I find, reflects society at large, so in the lineup one finds age discrimination as well as sexism against older women who sometimes struggle to pop up to our feet, as well as young girls who lack confidence and experience. Guys, with their natural, superior strength, blithely battle and out-paddle us for waves, cutting us off instead of waiting their turn.

Andree, a transplanted Californian and public school art teacher, is a blithe spirit, easygoing and generally unruffled by men's greater numbers and prissy looks of disdain. She just shrugs off the interference and goes for her next wave. On her long ride this morning she had shown what she can do, doubtless earning some grudging respect from the guys—not that she gives a whit what other people think.

Still, mellow as she is, Andree, like all the surfer women I know, sometimes gets frustrated and angry with repetitive male misbehavior, such as their shouldering

us off waves. We've learned to keep it to ourselves, though. We know better than to confront the men, who are often bigger, truculent, and surf in pairs or posses of bros. Instead, we'll do a little deconstructive venting just among ourselves, gathering in impromptu covens for a good cackle between waves.

That Saturday, happily, the guys were giving off relaxed, rather than testosterone-charged, vibes.

Andree and I surf in opposition to the size of our boards. On her round-nosed longboard, she sits amid the short-boarders at the inside lineup, closer to shore, where waves break more consistently over the shallow reef. That's how she picks off the waves the guys who sit deeper miss or fail to make, when the wave closes out, trapping them in the whitewater. On my shortboard, I sit on the outside, where longboarders traditionally wait for the bigger and less frequent set waves. This morning, when a set rolled in, I let the guys compete for the first and second waves, waited, and caught the third. It was steep, but the wall held up in the stiff offshore breeze, and I raced through three bracing sections to the invisible finishing line extending out from the dried-up Christmas tree planted in a rusty World War II standpipe on the reef.

"I made it to the Christmas tree" is a common boast at Suis, along with the generic "I got barreled (tubed)" you hear at almost any spot nowadays, even when the surf's so small you'd have to be a toddler to stand up in one. Which some toddlers do.

Next morning, Sunday, I was the only female amid nine guys. It was blown-out and smaller than the day before. The guys gave up, gradually, one by one, and as they went in, to my delight, they were replaced by women.

Debbie Millikan paddled out, having just come back from spring break with her family on Moloka'i, working

"I MADE IT TO THE CHRISTMAS TREE" IS A COMMON BOAST AT SUIS, ALONG WITH THE GENERIC "I GOT BARRELED (TUBED)" YOU HEAR AT ALMOST ANY SPOT NOW-ADAYS, EVEN WHEN THE SURF'S SO SMALL YOU'D HAVE TO BE A TODDLER TO STAND UP IN ONE. WHICH SOME TODDLERS DO.

← Unidentified surfer, Waikīkī Beach. Photo by Prayitno

on their organic farm. That's vacation for Debbie, a longtime environmental advo-cate and director of sustainability at Punahou School.

"Did I miss anything?" she asked in the timeless way of surfers everywhere. Going as far back as the "The Endless Summer" in the 1960s, our most common sayings are, "you shoulda been here yesterday" and "it was so much better an hour ago."

We discussed how surfing was either feast or famine: Just a few surfers like this morning, or thick crowds of regulars plus strangers, many of them beginners, so unschooled they pose a hazard by getting in the way.

The waves were picking up, offering some smallish but crisp, long lefts. Debbie missed a few, but then a set rolled in and she got the bomb, and when she came back out I told her so.

We were joined by Cristal Mortensen, who calls me her "mermaid sister," in her kabuki-white sunblock and trucker hat, her blond ponytail hanging out the back. A Pilates trainer and trauma therapist, Cristal looks super serious and Ninja intense in the lineup until she breaks into one of her grins and deep belly laughs.

These Suis regulars, plus charger Dodie Lau, mellow Ellen Farmer Freeman, moth-er-daughter duo Wisa and Lexi Miller and ocean ecologist Jonatha Giddens, are my impromptu surf buddies. Unlike most of the guys, we paddle out alone when-ever we can find free time in our work and family schedules. But in our unplanned meet-ups in the ocean, which happen several times a week, we form a happy little band of sisters. Like all friends, we have our occasional rivalries and fallings out, but when there's any trouble, we have each others' backs.

Sunday morning, Cristal greeted me with a smile. "Hey, Mermaid Sis, how's it?"

"Getting better," I said. "Less crowded than earlier."

"All right, good to hear!" She paddled deep, that is, towards the peak on the in-side lineup, scrambled onto a wave and popped up, her pink trucker cap bobbing up and down, over and under the back of the wave and cutting back, her board releasing a fountain of spray.

Debbie Millikan surfing at Suis (Suicides) off Diamond Head as seen from Mākālei Beach Park. Photo by Dennis Oda

# On a crowded summer evening a few years ago,

after waiting half an hour for my turn, I finally got a wave and took off deep, just under the overhead peak, and turned, flying down the line towards a big yellow sun setting in a mango-orange sky. It was a dream ride on a long, beautiful, open-faced wave when all at once, silhouetted against the sky, a large creature flailed and splashed atop the lip in my path, breaking my trance. I thought it was a turtle at first, then realized it was a guy paddling into the wave I was riding and about to drop in on me, committing the worst violation of surfing rules. But maybe it wasn't deliberate, maybe he hadn't seen me—it happens, I've been guilty of it myself. "Hey! Watch it," I cried, thinking he would pull back, but he kept paddling. I proned out, turning my board out of the wave and towards shore, but here he came, tumbling over the falls, his board slicing the air like a blade. Narrowly missing my head, it hit the front of my board with a bang. I heard a woman scream, and then the surfer himself fell on top of me.

We went under. I pushed his heavy body away, and after I fought my way to the surface and took a deep breath, I found myself staring into the eyes of a complete stranger. He wasn't local, that much was clear. He stared back. He didn't ask if I was all right, he didn't apologize. "You dropped in on me," I said, as I unfastened my leash to disentangle it from his. "That was bad. Don't do that."

He shrugged, got back on his board and paddled away. I felt my board; my fingers encountered shatters in the fiberglass and a deep, jagged gouge in the rail. I felt dazed and sick to my stomach. I remembered the woman's scream. Was that me?

No, it was Cristal, who race-paddled up to me with tears in her eyes, threw herself off her board, and hugged me. "Are you all right?" she asked.

"I'm fine," I said, trying to sound offhand.

"But that horrible sound when he hit you-—I thought he'd cracked your head. Are you sure you're okay?" She gently touched my head.

"I'm fine." Now I was crying, too. "But he dinged my board."

"Well, he has to pay for it! Where'd he go? Oh, look, he's hightailing it back to shore, the coward."

Cristal quickly took a wave and caught up with the miscreant, paddling alongside him to shore.

I waited until I recovered my equilibrium before catching a wave in. When I got to the beach park, she was waiting for me.

"I yelled at him all the way in," she said. "I told him Suis is an expert break and he had no business being out there. I told him he'd violated the rules and he had to pay to fix your board, but when we got to shore he sprinted off down the street!"

We laughed. We have never seen the guy again.

↑ At the entrance to Mākālei Beach Park on Oʻahu, (left to right) Melissa Kurpinski (balancing her longboard on her head), author Mindy Pennybacker, and Cristal Mortensen. Photo by Dennis Oda

I looked around. There were only females in the lineup. It's rare, but it happens. And the surf got better and better. The absence of males made me feel confident, energetic and relaxed, and I caught a lot more waves than usual.

Tired at last, I went in and, walking home, bumped into another Suis sister: tall, blond Sydney Iaukea in her leggings, prana top, and trucker hat, carrying her yoga mat after class in the nearby park. Syd has a PhD in political science from the University of Hawai'i at Mānoa and is author of *The Queen and I: A Story of Dispossessions and Reconnections in Hawai'i,* a memoir about her chance discovery that she was descended from Curtis Iaukea, who had been a faithful deputy to Hawai'i's last ruler, Queen Lili'uokalani, in the 1890s. She tells his story, and also covers the loss of Hawaiians' lands and suppression of their language, history, and culture after the 1893 illegal overthrow of the queen and annexation of the sovereign kingdom by the U.S.

THERE WERE ONLY FEMALES IN THE LINEUP. IT'S RARE, BUT IT HAPPENS. AND THE SURF GOT BETTER AND BETTER..

"So how is it?" Syd asked, meaning the surf.

"It's definitely better than it looks."

"Okay! I'm tired and hungry, but I'm going 'cause you said so," she said with a merry, ironic glint in her blue eyes.

"It'll probably get better with the dropping tide, so you could go home and eat first."

"Yeah, but then I'd lose my parking," she said with a laugh. "No worries! Water, energy bar, and I'm good to go."

Parking is in short supply on the urbanized island of O'ahu, especially in neighborhoods like mine, near the sea. When the waves are good, you see surfers changing out of their wet things behind their open car doors along the curbs.

What a nice morning, I thought as I walked Syd to her car and continued up the street. I saw my whole core group of surf sisters. Twelve years ago, I hadn't even known their names, having seen them out surfing only sporadically during brief

# Sisterhood is powerful,

to quote the famous rallying cry first heard in antiwar and women's liberation demonstrations in 1968. And thanks to the political action of our sisters, from the suffragettes of the early twentieth century to Hawai'i Congresswoman Patsy Mink, who in 1972 co-wrote and introduced Title IX of the Civil Rights Act, we enjoy myriad rights that women in traditional Hawai'i did not. We have the right to vote; to equal opportunity in education, employment and representation; to nondiscrimination in pay. Unlike women in traditional Hawaiian society, we can eat at the same table with men and we aren't denied certain 'ono, delicious foods because of our gender.

Nevertheless, in old Hawai'i, women had much more presence, respect, and power in the surf than we do today. It wasn't given to them by men. It was claimed as their due, going back to the surfing goddesses in the origin stories of the Hawaiian people who became Hawaiian when they discovered and named these islands and invented surfing. Sometimes, I find myself thinking I'd rather have a place in the waves than a place at the table. Then I come to my senses and remind myself that I and all my sisters have the right to both.

visits once or twice a year until I finally moved home after living in New York for twenty-seven years and before that in California and Iowa for eleven years. At first, when I started appearing at Suis day after day and they realized I wasn't leaving, I felt a chill. There's only so much room in a lineup and I understood that, even though I'd been surfing Suis since before most of them were born, I still had to earn my place.

Now, after twelve years, the tension has long since evaporated. We give each other waves and cheer one another on. We support each other, too, when faced by the aggression and insulting behavior too many male surfers show against females.

We'll sit off to one side, sympathize and vent about it, finding humor in how seriously men take themselves. Most times, a little merry laughter is all it takes to make the males slink away.

↑ Melissa Kurpinski (left) and Cristal Mortensen on their surfboards talk story before they paddle out to surf Suis (Suicides). Photo by Dennis Oda

← After surfing Suis (Suicides), veteran surfer Kim Heyer gives rookie Suis surfers a hug and kiss, (right to left) Isabel "Izzie" Cleofe, Wendy Sakuma, May Kamaka, and Mikayla Brennan at Mākālei Beach Park. Photo by Dennis Oda

# CHAPTER 4

# MĀKAHA SISTERS

Every wave is different and every lineup has its own personality. Male surfers at some spots cut women off even more than at Suis, while surfers in other areas are more welcoming and inclusive—if you know what you're doing and show the locals respect, that is.

It also doesn't hurt to be a local at a surf break, although it doesn't really help at Suis, a typical "town" break crowded with transients, surf samplers who have no interest in winning trust or building ties.

But there are some places in Hawai'i where it matters enormously who you are and whether you fit in.

← Mākaha Beach on O'ahu's West Side.

→ Mākaha Beach Park on Oʻahu.

↓ Mural in Mākaha.

Locals still reign at Mākaha Beach. Mākaha means fierce and its natural beauty and close-knit community are celebrated by the late Israel "Iz" Kamakawiwoʻole on his cover of John Denver's "Country Road," for which he wrote new lyrics:

ALMOST HEAVEN, WEST MAKAHA
HIGH-RIDGE MOUNTAIN, CRYSTAL-CLEAR BLUE WATER
ALL MY FRIENDS THEY'RE HANGING ON THE BEACH
YOUNG AND OLD AMONG THEM
FEEL THE OCEAN BREEZE.

The long white beach at the mouth of majestic Mākaha Valley lies at the end of the road on the Waiʻanae Coast on Oʻahu's West Side. Mākaha is an oceangoing community where traditional Hawaiian culture and values are kept alive by kūpuna, elders, and handed down through generations; a bronze bust of Iz stands on the beach.

MOST EVERYBODY WHO SURFS AT MĀKAHA KNOWS WHO'S FROM THERE AND WHO'S NOT.

— ANE BAKUTIS

"The hierarchy or the placement comes with who's local," said Ane Bakutis, a West Side native and business owner who grew up surfing Mākaha and now lives on Molokaʻi with her husband, a youth/community outreach coordinator for Queen Liliʻuokalani Trust, and their two children. Bakutis is the co-founder and daily operations manager of Kealopiko, an environmentally responsible apparel and home décor company that uses organic fibers and low-impact dyes, and draws images and inspiration from Hawaiian culture, history, and legend.

"Most everybody who surfs at Mākaha knows who's from there and who's not," Ane said. "You can't come sit way out here and catch the set wave if you're not from here. And if you try, a local guy will drop in on you."

Ane's sister Helena Bakutis-Kekau-la, age twenty-two, said that as a local female surfer at Mākaha, she felt being there was her birthright, one that received the respect of local males.

"I was raised at Mākaha Beach; my family was going there every time there was a nice swell to get tossed around in the surf," she said. "I started off bodyboarding on the same board with my dad before I turned one year old." Helena and Ane are daughters of surfer, conservationist, and writer Robert "Bunky" Bakutis.

A 2022 graduate in Hawaiian Studies from the University of Hawai'i at Mānoa, Helena added that for her, surfing is part of a lifestyle that embraces her Hawaiian background as well as the local community, the 'āina and kai and the species that inhabit them, and her own natural tendency to enjoy going with the flow.

The latter is reflected in her preference for longboarding over shortboarding. Shortboards allow surfers to perform stunts such as thrusting the tip of the board above the lip of the wave, launching themselves completely into the air, and aggressively "shredding" the waves with powerful, "hacking" turns.

"I love longboarding because it's the more graceful and easygoing way to surf, not so, like, high performance," Helena says. "You can kind of relax on the waves, show more style."

Helena was also part of a neighborhood kids' surf group. "Growing up, I had two really good friends who were girls and a couple boys my age. We wouldn't really plan to get together, but we'd all be at the beach at the same time and meet each other out in the lineup. It was like our playground."

She had teachers, too, among the kūpuna who oversaw and enforced the rules of the surf, and who looked out for the safety of the keiki and encouraged them.

# The beachboys taught surfing,

gave canoe and catamaran rides at the gentle break called Canoes in Waikīkī, played and sang Hawaiian music, caught fish and held lūʻau, and otherwise kept Hawaiian culture and aloha alive in the epicenter of tourism. Few beachboys in the grand old tradition still work the beach; one of the last is Didi Robello, who in 1983 took over Aloha Beach Services, his father Harry Robello's beach concession in front of the Royal Hawaiian Hotel.

Harry Robello was one of the original Waikīkī beachboys who

← The famed Beachboys in Waikīkī line up behind Duke Kahanamoku and pose in front of the old Moana hotel pier, circa 1920. Photo by Ray Jerome Baker. Hawaiʻi State Archives

started working with visitors staying at the Moana Surfrider and Royal Hawaiian hotels, the first two hotels on the beach. Robello worked and played alongside Duke Kahanamoku, the great-uncle of Didi Robello, whose grandfather was Bill Kahanamoku.

"A lot of the uncles and aunties love to see the next generation coming up," Helena said. "In Wai'anae, it's very family and community oriented, and my dad is good friends with all the beachboys, so they would recognize me as his daughter, encourage me to go on their waves, or catch a big wave they saw was lining up perfectly for me."

Historically there has been a close connection between Mākaha and Waikīkī surfers, who competed in the Mākaha International Surfing Championships from 1954-1971, which were considered to be the unofficial world championships, according to Matt Warshaw's *Encyclopedia of Surfing*.

Surfers tend to be migratory, following the waves that change with the seasons: Spring/summer brings swells to the islands' south shores, while winter is the time big waves pound the north and northwestern shores, like Mākaha. When the renowned watermen known as the Waikīkī beachboys came to surf Mākaha, Helena got to know them through her dad.

Aloha Kathie, mucho Aloha. MDrz 2/22

↑ Young Mākaha surfers with veteran surfer, Kathy Terada. (left to right) Kalia Keaulana, Taiahni Keaulana, Kathy Terada, AiLana Barboza, Kira Keaulana, and Bianca Paragas. Photo by Marcelo Diaz Rodriguez

As a young man in the 1950s, Richard "Buffalo" Keaulana worked as a beachboy, commuting thirty-five miles from the West Side to Waikīkī until he married and returned home to live and raise a family. Every winter for forty-five years, except during the Covid-19 pandemic, the Keaulana family and friends have held the annual Buffalo Big Board Classic, a weekend of surf contests and games that raises funds for community needs.

While Helena learned from Buffalo and the other beachboy uncles when to take a wave, she also learned when not to go. She learned to wait her turn and defer to others with priority, including kūpuna, as dictated by surf etiquette. Growing up in Hawai'i, kids learn to read the silent vocabulary of facial expressions and ges-

Rell Sunn, "The Queen of Makaha," 1983.
Photo by Dennis Oda/Honolulu Star-Bulletin

tures such as a chin-up or a nod. So it was with Helena and other favored keiki of the West Side, and the uncles. "They cheer you on, maybe more than give you the eye not to go."

Helena's role models and inspirations are two older Hawaiian women. She grew up with the legend and legacy of the late Rell Sunn, known as the Queen of Mākaha, who had been a state junior surfing champion and world champion longboarder, Mākaha lifeguard, and advocate for children's welfare, community health, and women's rights.

"I grew up entering in Aunty Rell's Menehune Surf Contest event, which was all the kids getting together to have a fun competition day at Mākaha," Helena said, referring to an annual event Sunn founded for local children in 1975. Since Sunn's death, in January 1998, it has been continued by her family and community sponsors as a fundraiser for the nonprofit Rell Sunn Educational Fund which was established by her daughter, Jan Sunn-Careira.

Although she was born after Sunn's death, Helena regards the Queen of Mākaha as a constant, familiar presence in the sea. "I definitely enjoy her style of surfing, which I've seen in photos and videos, and her menehune contest," Helena said, "and the long-lasting imprint she had on Mākaha is carried on by her family."

↓ Rell Sunn with Nancy Emerson and competition sponsor Joe DiPaulo (left) at the Hang Ten Women's International Pro Surfing Championship in 1979. Photo by John Titchen/Honolulu Star-Bulletin

No surprise, Helena's second idol is a contemporary legend, five-time world champion Carissa Moore, winner at age twenty-eight of the first Olympic gold medal for women's surfing. Moore, now thirty, has established a nonprofit organization to support girls' confidence and self-esteem in pursuing their dreams, and advocates to make surfing an interscholastic sport in Hawai'i public schools.

Helena admires Moore as an example of the best in surfing and of the prog-

↓ (left to right) Jeannie Chesser; son Todd Chesser; Buffalo Keaulana; and son Brian Keaulana, at China's Longboard Surfing Contest in Waikīkī, 1986. Photo by Dennis Oda/ Honolulu Star-Bulletin

Competitors in the 44th Annual Buffalo Big Board Surfing Classic, 2022, in Mākaha.

Tandem boogie board event.

→ Helena Bakutis and nephew Kahiki ride team bodyboard. Courtesy Bakutis family

↑ Tandem surfers (top two photos). One of the rated positions is to lie down on the surfboard while riding the waves like a cockroach (bottom photo).

ress women are making towards equity throughout society. "In the Olympics, seeing Carissa, powerful and graceful at the same time—that's what surfing stands for."

Moore, she added, is a representative for all women, for being "strong and fearless and putting up a good competition towards men, as well."

While there are still fewer than half as many women as men in competitive surfing, "I think women are advancing in the form of getting more brave and confident, testing their limits, being able to try and do the more complicated maneuvers as men do," Helena said. "Because of Carissa's example, other women think they can do the same and perform at the same level."

She stressed it was "very important" that women and men get parity of compensation across the board, from the same salary to the same prize money, noting that since 2019, women professional surfers have been receiving equal prize money to men.

Speaking for herself, though, "I've never been the competitive type, I just go out and have fun."

> IT SHOULD BE RECOGNIZED THAT HAWAI'I IS DEFINITELY THE BIRTHPLACE OF SURFING, FOR WHICH IT MAYBE DOESN'T GET ENOUGH CREDIT.
>
> — HELENA BAKUTIS-KEKAULA

Reminded that she had been competitive enough to win second place in the annual Buffalo's Big Board Classic at Mākaha in 2022, she laughed. "This year, I've been able to surf more, maybe getting better," she said, lauding her close friend Ha'a Keaulana, Buffalo Keaulana's granddaughter, for winning the women's division.

What she valued most about the Big Board Classic, Helena said, was that it benefited charity and provided a good platform for sharing Mākaha while having challenging fun.

"It should be recognized that Hawai'i is definitely the birthplace of surfing, for which it maybe doesn't get enough credit," Helena said. Most of all, she hoped people would take care of the natural resources that sustain surfing.

"I would love to see people giving back to the beaches that they enjoy a lot," she said. "In Mākaha, not just environmentalists but regular locals are also doing beach cleanup days. It's about maintaining some part of the beach, planting native plants, keeping its natural beauty, because a lot of erosion is happening and climate change may be changing the reef."

At Mākaha, just before the end of the road, two-lane Farrington Highway runs across the sands, splitting the beach in two. When high tides and big waves strike this hard infrastructure, the backwash claws away sand causing beach erosion that is getting worse with the sea level rise due to climate change. For decades, Buffalo Keaulana, his son Brian Keaulana, a big-wave safety instructor and former lifeguard, Helena's father Bunky Bakutis, and other West Side residents have been pressing the state to move the highway and the crumbling bridge that carries it over to Mākaha Stream, inland and up the valley.

"Mākaha is such a good place to gather, we want to fight for it to be well-maintained and preserved for future generations," Helena said. What also makes Mākaha special, she said, is the way multiple generations surf together.

"My dad, it's just incredible to me that he's still surfing at seventy-seven. My sister's kids are thirteen and nine, just starting to really get confident, and we all get to ride waves together, play around—have a good laugh, or an exciting moment seeing the kids do a new trick."

Helena's sister, Ane Bakutis, agreed their 'ohana surf outings are the best. "What's really fun, no matter what size the waves are, is being out there with Helena, my dad, my kids—three generations. It's so awesome," she said. "Not only are we all stoked to be with each other as a family, but to be in the water surfing. So it's double stoke."

The intergenerational surfing stoke extends far beyond their nuclear family. "The thing with Mākaha that's different than most other places is, it's not just about surfing: Your surfing beach family becomes like your personal family," Ane said. "There's families, we're at the beach all the time, see each other every day, bring each other fish they've caught."

Given the twenty-four-year age gap between herself and Helena, Ane—the two are half-sisters, from different mothers—feels she helped to raise Helena in many ways, "almost like a prelude to having my own kids. I wanted to make sure she had a similar experience with the ocean and surfing that I did growing up, and she did. She was just like this fish from birth. The ocean is where she feels most comfortable."

The young Helena had no fear, Ane said. "We would swim half a mile out in Mākaha when she was four years old and she loved it. I would pick her up from her mom's home in town, and we would surf on the same boogie board."

But while the sisters were both confident water girls from an early age, Ane perceived a generational difference in their experiences in the Mākaha lineup. Unlike Helena, Ane said, she had not felt accepted.

"When I was growing up, it wasn't that way at all," she said regarding the lack of gender discrimination her younger sister took for granted. "When I was a girl, it was definitely male dominated, with just a handful of wahine in the water surfing."

By the time Helena started out, there were many more women in the water, Ane said, noting times had changed. "Helena grew up in the *Blue Crush* era," she said, referring to the 2002 film about women surfers on O'ahu's North Shore who face harassment in

← Left to right: Ane Bakutis, son Kahiki, father Bunky, daughter Poohini (foreground) and sister Helena Bakutis on Mākaha Beach. Photo courtesy Bakutis family

← Helena Bakutis, front, and Maili Kalama ride tandem Bullyboard at the Buffalo Big Board Surfing Classic in 2020. Photo by Robert Bunky Bakutis

and out of the water from men. Kate Bosworth stars as a surfer suffering with PTSD after a near-death wipeout, who masters her fears and rides a big tube at Banzai Pipeline in a contest, scoring a perfect ten.

The film also stars Michelle Rodriguez and real-life Hawaiian surfers Sanoe Lake and Coco Ho, and features pro surfers Keala Kennelly, a big-wave world champion from Kaua'i, Kate Skarratt, Megan Abubo, four-time world champion Lisa Andersen, renowned barrel-rider Rochelle Ballard, and seven-time world champion Lane Beachley.

"Helena actually was in *Blue Crush*. There's a clip at the very end of a little baby on boogie board; that's her with our dad," Ane added.

While the film showed women mastering big, dangerous North Shore waves, its message of female empowerment was undercut in the climactic scene in which pro surfer Noah Johnson, an obvious man in a long-hair wig and a bikini, appeared as Bosworth's stunt double in her triumphant Pipeline tube ride.

What kept Ane's confidence up in the pre-*Blue Crush* era twenty years earlier, when there were fewer females in the lineup, was the encouragement and protection of a group of older women known as the Westside Wahines; members included Al Momoa, Brooke Holt-Pennell, Dalani Tanahy, Claudia Woo, Cathy Sipe, Rell Sunn, Tinky Leach, Haze Pave, Pua Mokuau, and Kathy Terada.

"The Westside Wahines (held) the first all-wahine surfing competition at Mākaha in the mid-1990s," Ane said.

Ane felt especially close to Rell Sunn and the late Pua Mokuau, who worked in tandem with Sunn as the two first female lifeguards at Mākaha Beach.

"Pua was just a super strong, beautiful Hawaiian bodybuilder, breaking a lot of glass ceilings for Hawaiian women throughout Hawai'i as Auntie Rell did, too. Pua liked to surf bigger waves. She liked it when it was six feet (Hawaiian measure, with twelve-foot wave faces) or bigger. Auntie Rell Sunn, loved three to four feet, perfect Mākaha—she was amazing, but also a fair weather surfer, and of course the superstar. But having all these other women, the Westside Wahines, backing her up made it possible for her to support all us kids, pushing us girls to surf."

But it wasn't just surfing. The women taught the girls that surfing, like hula and spearfishing, was just one of many interconnected parts in the holistic, traditional lifestyle they had been trying to learn about and revive. The 1960s and 70s saw the birth of a Hawaiian renaissance in which activists young and old fought to restore their native language, music, dance, religion, farming and fisheries, and healing and protection of ecosystems, shrines and other ancient sites.

"We cared for our beach and 'āina," write Westside Wahines founding member, Claudia Woo, on the "Legendary Surfers" Facebook page, noting the group provided trash cans for Mākaha Beach, held beach clean-ups, and educated girls about outlets for health awareness and cancer screenings.

"With Pua we danced hula, and we had the privilege of helping to restore an old heiau in the back of Mākaha Valley," Ane said. "That was just an amazing time, doing something to perpetuate our culture and preserve this special site. Pua had a way about her

↑ Pua Mokuau. Photo courtesy Kathy Terada

that was so peaceful and so full of aloha, always smiling. She had that twinkle in her eye, made you just feel at ease and comfortable with anything you were doing, in the ocean or anywhere."

Mokuau died of cancer in June 1997, seven months before Sunn, and was commemorated in an obituary written by Ane and Helena's father, Bunky Bakutis, then a reporter for the *Honolulu Advertiser*.

Knowing the Westside Wahines had her back, the young Ane didn't let the guys intimidate her as she fought for her share of waves. "I think most women surfers are at least a little bit feminist," she said. "Whether you like it or not, you have to be a little bit aggressive—just getting a wave is competition in itself, because you gotta outpaddle the next guy to get on the wave first."

She entered junior surf competitions, but there were no girls' divisions, so girls surfed against the boys. "When I would beat a boy, he would be upset, you could just see it on his face." She remembered the pride she felt in one of her girlfriends, who routinely won events and "left a lot of guys crying in her wake."

Although she lives and works on Moloka'i, Ane comes home to surf with her family at Mākaha whenever she can. She finds not much has changed, except now there are more female surfers and she's become one of the older wahine teaching respect to packs of clueless boys who view her as an outsider.

SURFING IS PART OF OUR CULTURE, NOT ONLY SOMETHING HANDED DOWN FROM OUR ANCESTORS BUT PART OF WHO WE ARE AS HAWAIIANS IN HAWAI'I. IT'S A SPIRITUAL CONNECTION TO NATURE.

— ANE BAKUTIS

"Because I don't live in Mākaha anymore, one of the hardest things about going home is all the ruthless kids dropping in on me," she said. "If they do it once, okay, but twice, I'm gonna tell 'em, 'Eh, don't drop in on your auntie!'" She also scolds them for cutting off any kūpuna, elderly surfers to whom respect and courtesy must be shown.

"You gotta fight for your waves and you gotta call guys off the wave, you get your position in the whole hierarchy of surfing there, but it all works out," she said. "My husband now tells me I catch too many waves when I go home," she added with a laugh. "He says, 'You gotta let someone else catch waves.'"

For her own children, a boy of thirteen and a girl of ten, "I think it's really good for both of them to have a mom who surfs," she said. "For my son, seeing mom charge some big waves is 'oh, wow, I can do that, I'm a guy'. My daughter, who's just coming out of being a little bit scared of bigger waves than four feet, can think, 'Okay, I can do this, like my mom.'"

As her children try wave riding maneuvers, they've started to critique her rides. "They go, 'Mom, how come you didn't do a cutback over there?'"

"There are points where you get scared, but at the end of day, you go back and surf," she added, noting that overcoming your fear and paddling back out is the work part. "It's not just fun."

# Talking story with Ane and Helena,

one hears that from their perspective, heʻe nalu is more than recreation. If it sometimes feels like work paddling out, as wave after wave beats you back on a rising swell and tide, or terror when you paddle over a ledge and drop down a watery cliff, swooping on a rail to possible oblivion, that's because it is.

The concepts of work and fear, however, clash with the casual meme of recreational surfers, especially guys, who want to make it all seem easy, a byproduct of their natural talent and strength. It's not cool to appear to care too much, although paradoxically it's okay to battle over small, insignificant waves, lose your temper, and vent on girls.

Supplanting the use of "sick" as slang for a great wave, "fun" is the word of choice surfers use to describe a good surf these days. "It was fun! There were some fun waves," they chirp as they greet one another coming and going, over and over, every day.

But to Ane Bakutis, Helena Bakutis-Kekaula, Uʻilani Macabio, and other Hawaiian women, surfing is serious and deep, a practice that approaches a rite as they face and acknowledge the mysterious, changing moods of the all-powerful sea.

"Surfing is part of our culture, not only something handed down from our ancestors but part of who we are as Hawaiians in Hawaiʻi. It's a spiritual connection to nature." Ane said.

# CHAPTER 5

# TONGG'S

When they hear of "one brief shining moment," most people think of Camelot. A very few, a happy few, think of Tongg's. For almost a decade, the Tongg's Gang enjoyed something approaching the community spirit that's still alive at Mākaha. Unlike the residents of that storied shore, we lacked a single, unifying heritage: We were an eclectic mixture of public and private school kids of Hawaiian, Chinese, Japanese, Korean, Filipino, haole (Caucasian) and hapa (mixed-race) descent, from both traditional and broken homes. But we were all teenagers who felt a deep, loyal comradeship and shared a mad passion for the surf.

← Yoshie Shimabayasha carefully navigates the slippery stairs with her surfboard at Tongg's near Kapi'olani Park, O'ahu. Photo by Dennis Oda

From the late 1960s to the mid 1970s, we lived and surfed in a world of our own—a small, sleepy, rundown neighborhood by the sea that still seems frozen in time, although many of the original 1920s cottages have been replaced by high-rise condominium buildings and mega-mansions used for illegal, short-term vacation rentals. Tongg's Beach is named for Ruddy Fah Tongg, who bought a beachfront home in 1946 and developed the high-rise Kainalu apartment building on his lot in the early 1960s, according to John Clark in *Hawai'i Place Names*.

This pocket neighborhood, which I only recently learned is officially named Diamond Head Terrace, not the "Tongg's neighborhood" of common parlance, lies wedged between the sprawling mansions of Diamond Head and the green open spaces of Kapi'olani Park, which stretches a mile along the shoreline and ends at Waikīkī's hotels, busy streets, groomed beaches, and long, glassy, perfect waves.

A surfer catches a wave at Tongg's, 2017.
Photo by Cindy Ellen Russell/Honolulu Star-Advertiser

Our Diamond Head waves are choppier than Waikīkī's, torn up by the prevailing side-shore winds from the east. But when we were young, we loved these waves because they were all ours. From east to west, our neighborhood breaks stretch for half a mile, encompassing the breaks of Sleepy Hollows, Suicides, Channels, Graveyards, Radicals, The Winch, Zeros, Tongg's, Ricebowls, Hotels, and the mysterious break called Noplace by some, Nowheres by others.

Suicides, Graveyards, Radicals, and the Winch closed out when the waves reached higher than four feet, when we'd paddle out to the deep, blue water breaks of Channels, Zeros, and Ricebowls. Over time, the boys in the gang taught me the lineup and profiles of the waves in each break except Sleepy Hollows and Noplace/Nowheres, whose thick, sloping waves didn't interest shortboarders at the time. They started me out at Tongg's, which was known, then as now, as a beginner break, with the sincere conviction that I would soon be surfing at their level. They treated me as someone of equal potential and were soon taking me out into the challenging waves at Suis and even Ricebowls, which were well beyond my level.

SURFING WAS SERIOUS, INTENSELY FOCUSED PLAY FOR THE BOYS OF THE TONGG'S GANG.

I was hapless. Although I followed them eagerly and tried to follow instructions, I ended up wiping out and swimming for my board, more than I actually rode it (this was before surf leashes arrived on the scene in 1971).

This was no surprise to me. A shy, bookish child, I was a failure at every sport we played in P.E. class, as well as at the President's Fitness Test inaugurated in 1961 by the Kennedy Administration. I could never do a single pull-up. The only exercise I enjoyed was free swimming and bodysurfing in the ocean—aimless play, an escape from the academic and social pressures of Punahou School, a private college preparatory academy.

Surfing was serious, intensely focused play for the boys of the Tongg's Gang. They had grown up surfing, and the long, incessant paddling had shaped their bodies into wedges: broad shoulders, deeply muscled backs and chests; latissimus dorsi like wings; narrow waists; barely-there hips; the long, skinny, almost vestigial legs of waterbirds.

My back was bony as a chicken's, with jutting shoulder blades. My torso was straight and flat as an ironing board, and my arms were skinny and weak. However, thanks to going barefoot all my life, I did have wide lūʻau feet which were good for balance, with spreading toes like a lizard's that clung to the waxed deck of my board. Thanks to my feet, I excelled in at least one physical endeavor at school: the balance beam.

"Come on," the boys would cry, paddling into a protective wing formation around me and shooting warning glares at potential droppers-in. "Hurry up! It's your wave. Paddle, paddle, paddle harder!" they'd scream, which flustered me. If I missed the wave, and I usually did, they'd groan and sigh. But they never gave up hope, and neither did I.

It was more relaxing to surf with other girls, school friends, who liked to hang out at our house near the beach in summer. A family friend had given us a used longboard, so I had a spare for friends to use. Other girls instantly understood the dichotomy between genders in the waves. We were smaller and lighter than most of the boys, softer bodied and more vulnerable to accidental blows from boards. Our developing bodies felt sore and tender at times, making us hesitant to go for it on a big, sketchy looking wave. Our protruding hipbones got bruised paddling, our long hair got tangled and sometimes wrapped around our faces during a wipeout, so when we fought our way back to the surface it was hard to breathe. Plus, bikini tops and bottoms got yanked halfway off when we wiped out or got tumbled trying to paddle out through breaking waves. And, paddling out through sets, we hated and feared having waves break on us and tossing us about as we clung to our boards.

Still, we laughed off our accidents, cheered each others' circus aerialist freefalls as well as the occasional, complete ride, and best of all there was no pressure. The girls weren't as serious as the boys, who seemed to be constantly watching and mentally scoring everyone's rides, including their own.

Now and then, the boys in the gang would lose patience. "Stop talking, pay attention," they'd tell me—good advice, it was dangerous if you didn't look out for waves. "Get serious!" they'd add with inadvertently tetchy, disapproving expressions that for some reason reminded me of my grandmother's admonishments about lack of table manners and never failed to make me laugh.

Two of my friends were on the swim team and had the long, strong muscles, endurance, and speed that are an invaluable help in surfing. They had grown up in

→ Lani Marumoto (eleven years old) with her surfboard after surfing with her dad, Jay Marumoto, at Tongg's. Photo by Dennis Oda

← The public beach access to Tongg's.

↓ A young girl paddles out to compete in the Menehune competition during Duke Kahanamoku OceanFest, 2015, at Queen's Beach in Waikīkī.

Hawaiian families who spent a lot of time in the ocean, where they felt at home. Still, while they enjoyed the rush of surfing, they were trained to slice efficiently back and forth through the flat, predictable waters of pools, and as the novelty wore off, they tired of getting tossed about by wild, ever-changing waves. As summer ended and varsity swim practice resumed, they gave up surfing.

"Too much water!" one of them said with a shrug and a laugh.

"Too much of a good thing," I said, and she agreed, but I understood that, as a competitive athlete, she couldn't risk overtiring herself.

More than thirty years later, after we'd both lived on the mainland for some time, my friend and I took our sons to Tongg's Beach for a surf lesson. I was the teacher, while my friend relaxed on the beach with a book. "I know it's sad, but after all those years of competitive swimming, I eventually lost the desire to go in the water," she said.

The boys, though, were thirteen—the same age as she and I had been when we started surfing—and happy as monk seal cubs. On antique longboards, they

↑ Surfer Hana Harrison at Tongg's. Photo by
Craig T. Kojima/Honolulu Star-Advertiser          74

paddled after me over the sharp, shallow reef of Inside Tongg's. Despite my directions, they paddled too slowly and didn't pay attention to their position on the boards, lying too far back and with their legs splayed and feet dragging. More focused on conversing than their environment, they were drifting down current. I heard myself shouting, "Stop talking, pay attention!"

We finally got outside to deeper water where we sat up on our boards. Now they felt motivated and listened and paddled as hard as they could; naturally strong and coordinated, they both caught waves all the way in, springing to their feet. I took a wave, but as we paddled out another, bigger set came, the waves rising up to axe down on us. The boys were too far inside to push through the faces of the waves before they broke, and it was too shallow to roll under and let the boards shield their bodies from the impact. So wave after wave broke on their heads and shoulders, pounding them hard, but to my amazement, they emerged from the foam each time with delighted smiles and laughter. I realized they were actually enjoying what to me had been the most grievous of punishments at their age. These were boys. They were grinning like two crocodiles. They were having fun.

"Pay attention. Get serious," the boys of the Tongg's Gang used to scold me, but I wasn't going to scold my young son, Rory, and his friend. Rory, like his father, is a strong, committed bodysurfer, but he didn't share my drive to master riding a board. The boys in the gang had seen my drive and the competitive spirit I suppressed out of fear of failure, whether in academics, music, or sports. I was reluctant to face how much I really cared and wanted to shine. The Tongg's Gang had pushed me to be open about my desire to achieve excellence and to go for it. They had been good teachers.

Surfing, with all its public setbacks, humiliations, and gravity-defying triumphs, toughened me up, making

# Females were a small minority

in the surf in the 1960s, just as we were in law firms and executive suites. We knew society was poised for change: Betty Friedan's boat-rocking *The Feminine Mystique* was published in 1966, the year the National Organization for Women was founded. Still, as an insecure young member of a minority stigmatized as the weaker sex, instead of seeking solidarity, I held myself separate from the other surfer girls. I was competing with them for limited space in the boys' world of the waves. My goal was to surf like a boy in order to be accepted by the ruling, male majority.

At the same time, whenever I got a good ride, I knew it was because I was surfing like a girl, that is, like myself. I was at one with the speed, shape, and rhythm of the wave, expressing myself and not thinking about boys or anyone else at all, unless they got in my way.

me more persistent in striving for my goals and less concerned about what people thought. It helped me to be more competitive in academics, speak up in class, and win leadership positions in student government and publications.

Sometimes I wonder if I might have studied harder, achieved more professionally and made more money if I hadn't spent so much time chasing waves—the answer is probably yes, but I can't conceive of having lived life to the fullest without my time in the waves.

Occasionally, when I was starting out, other girls would appear at Tongg's. Some of them were as good as the best boys at paddling and riding waves, but most, like me, were of intermediate skills. Then there were the sad-eyed, clueless beginners who could scarcely paddle, escorted out by boyfriends who soon abandoned them. I never spoke with any of these other girls; I couldn't seem to break out of my isolation. Maybe it made me feel special.

My surfing solitude ended during my last two years of high school, when I became friends with a classmate, Gayle Keani Reiner, who surfed at Tongg's. She was a gentle, softspoken girl with dark, sparkling eyes, brown hair, and an olive complexion. She was also a hard-bodied, broad-shouldered, power surfer. We'd do homework at my house after school and then go surfing until dark. Keani was qui-

et, alert, and always smiling in the ocean, through which she moved as naturally as a dolphin. She reminded me of a Hawaiian princess or goddess, such as Māmala, an avid surfer who was said to be part-woman, part mo'o, or sea dragon, and could take either form.

Keani learned to sail at age seven and paddled for a Hawaiian outrigger canoe club in her teens. In 1976, she and Penny Martin became the first women to crew on the *Hōkūle'a* ("Star of Gladness"), the Polynesian Voyaging Society's oceangoing canoe built by volunteers like herself. A lodestar of the Hawaiian cultural renaissance, the double-hulled canoe, using traditional Polynesian celestial navigation,

↑ Keani Reiner. Photo courtesy Shea Reiner

Surfing Tongg's. Photo by Dennis Oda

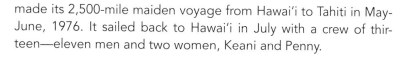

made its 2,500-mile maiden voyage from Hawai'i to Tahiti in May-June, 1976. It sailed back to Hawai'i in July with a crew of thirteen—eleven men and two women, Keani and Penny.

The homeward crossing recreated the voyage made by the Tahitian explorers who discovered the Hawaiian islands a millennium before, proving that Hawai'i had been settled by explorers from the South Pacific who deliberately sailed north against prevailing currents, discrediting the long-held theory that the settlement of Hawai'i happened by accident, when Polynesians on rafts drifted westward with the currents from Rapa Nui.

After we graduated from high school, Keani moved to Kaua'i where she got her captain's license and sailed throughout the South Pacific. She married and had a son, but she died of cancer in 1994, at age forty-two. Recently, I happened upon a brief video of her reading aloud excerpts from the log she'd kept during the 1976 *Hōkūle'a* trip. There was footage of her at the helm of *Hōkūle'a*, wearing a green Tahitian bikini in the sunshine and foul weather gear in the cold and rain. It was moving to hear her fresh, youthful voice again after so many years.

"Passed a huge school of porpoise," she wrote on the fourteenth day out. "How I would love to live like them."

She also read from her entry about a night watch she kept towards the end of the twenty-two-day voyage, when the crew members were exhausted, cranky, and yearning for home and privacy. "Polaris visible now," she read in her soft voice. "Cold, wet night. Hear the sweep hitting our hulls, the wind flying by, waves splashing over the deck, the excitement of the crew on deck. *Hōkūle'a* is alive."

Keani was strong, courageous, patient, gentle, and kind. Her eyes and smile radiated aloha. Many Hawaiian women say when they surf they feel the comforting presence of loved ones who have died. Sometimes when I am surfing after sunset, and a tinge of fear sets in, I like to think that Keani is somewhere nearby, a guardian spirit at home in the sea she loved.

# CHAPTER 6

# THE JOY OF SURFING

Dim, ghostly shapes in the chill, predawn dark, they stand in swimsuits, barefoot or in rubber slippers beside their cars at beach parks from Hawaiʻi Kai to ʻĀina Haina, on the cliffs above Diamond Head Beach, or the bifurcated strip of Kalākaua Avenue that stretches along the oceanfront of Kapiʻolani Park near Waikīkī. They're busy, no-nonsense, taking out and waxing their surf boards, tying back their hair, pulling on wetsuits or rash guards and paddling out before the sun rises over the mounds of Koko Head and Diamond Head.

← Early morning surf session.

They don't have much time. An hour or two later, in the early morning light, they are rinsing off at park showers or hoses or with jugs of water kept in their cars, putting their boards away and, behind open car doors and draped towels, changing into suits, dresses and high heels, or scrubs and sneakers, brushing their hair and putting on makeup. They are the workaday women surfers of O'ahu's South Shore.

Among them is Honolulu journalist and mother Catherine (Cat) Toth Fox, who has been paddling out to the surf on her longboard at 4:45 a.m., nearly every day for more than twenty years.

But why? Why do girls and women love surfing? What do we get out of it? Do we surf differently and for different reasons than men?

When asked why they surf, most of the girls and women I interviewed seemed surprised, even taken aback. "Oh, wow, what a question! I've never really thought about it—let me think for a minute," was a typical first response.

Melissa Kurpinski walking along Diamond Head Road in the early morning on her way to Suis (Suicides). Photo by Dennis Oda

But once they started talking surf, they had plenty to say.

For Cat, a Kalihi native who participated in school athletics, surfing is far more than a sport. It's a total lifestyle she treasures because, unlike most other activities you can pursue in adult years, surfing is "just pure play."

Kaimukī resident Cappy Makaiau, eleven, who started surfing at age four, was one of the few who answered the question without a pause. "I really like the ocean because it's really refreshing. I like surfing because when I catch a wave it's super fun, it just brings you in," she said as she sat under a banyan tree in Mākālei Beach Park and studied the waves at Suis, her hazel eyes shining with light reflected off the sea.

"I also skate, which is sort of like the same thing—they're both on a board, and the (skate) ramp goes down like a wave," she added. "But the difference is that skating, you know, it's set in concrete, while in the ocean, every single wave is different—some have more of a curve, some are more vertical."

With her friend and classmate, Ella, Cappy takes surf lessons from a family friend who drives them to different, beginner-friendly spots all around O'ahu, including the North Shore. In town, she also surfs at Kewalos and Ala Moana Beach Park with her father, Jarad Makaiau, and Ella and her dad.

↑ Cappy Makaiau at Mākālei Beach Park. Photo by Dennis Oda

UH student May Kamaka and her friends at Mākālei Beach Park to go surfing at Suis (Suicides) on O'ahu. Photo by Dennis Oda

Asked whether she thought people surfed differently according to gender, Cappy shook her head. "Boys, girls, it's kind of the same," she said. "Gender doesn't really matter because everybody's trying the same thing, to catch a wave."

Okay. Surfing's exciting, refreshing and fun. But are there other reasons girls and women surf? The answer is a resounding yes. For many, there's the social life.

"I love surfing because I'm happy being close to my friends, looking out for each other and cheering each others' rides," said Wendy Sakuma, a native of Palo Alto, California, who took up surfing a year and a half ago with her friends at the University of Hawai'i, Mānoa. "I haven't been taught a lesson, I just copy all my friends," she said, adding that the four students organize regular Sunday surf expeditions of up to twenty friends, including experienced surfers, to different breaks around O'ahu.

For Cat, there are the long-term relationships she's formed in the water over time. "In what other sport are you sitting together in the same spot for two hours?" she

May Kamaka, Wendy Sakuma, Isabel "Izzie" Cleofe, and Mikayla Brennan assessing the surf at Suis before they paddle out. Photo by Dennis Oda

Catherine Toth Fox surfing at Waikīkī Beach. Photo by Dave Miyamoto

said. "It is our time, we talk in between waves, and that's how they became some of my closest—not friends, necessarily, as they're twenty to thirty years older than me—they're more like family."

At the same time, "I like that it's fairly superficial, because it's too hard to carry on a full conversation—a wave comes and you're always like, wait, wait, hold that thought!"

Cat's surfing 'ohana happens to be all male, except for one other woman, reflecting the overall gender ratio for the sport. The oldest in the group is eighty, and Cat has joined them and their spouses for everything from breakfasts to surf trips as far as Cloudbreak, Fiji, or to simply unwind in Las Vegas. She's seen them go through marriages, retirement, divorces.

# Before I started surfing with the Tongg's Gang,

I was taught the basics by my "calabash" uncle Clarence "Shippy" Kealoha, husband of my mom's best friend, Pauline, with their eldest children Nalani and Kekahili, who took us out to Queen's Surf in Waikīkī. Uncle Shippy taught us the rules of etiquette and safety: take your turn, don't go for every wave; paddle back out around the shoulders of the waves, not straight through the impact zone in front of the peak where the waves are breaking and surfers are taking off; and turning turtle—rolling underwater and holding your board as a shield over your head—if you were trapped in the path of an approaching surfer or big wave about to break. Uncle Shippy taught us to be friendly and respectful to everyone, most of all the old-timers, the kūpuna, some of whom, he said, had been old when he first paddled out to learn as a boy. "Eh, Shippy," they'd say as we joined the crowded lineup, and he'd raise his chin and straighten his shoulders as he replied to them by name. The old-timers sat much farther out than anyone else—halfway out to the horizon, it seemed—on longboards called tankers, big as boats.

And they dominated. Some of them still do, while other, new kūpuna have taken the places of those who no longer surf. On their high-floating boards, the kūpuna are able to paddle onto waves before they began to break, asserting priority over everybody waiting farther inside. But "go kids," they'd occasionally say in soft, detached tones of noblesse oblige, pointing with a flick of their fingers as if dropping crumbs for birds, as we gawked, stunned to be addressed by

*Aerial drone shot of surfers ready to catch early morning waves at Waikīkī Beach.*

overeager and dropped in on their waves without permission, the wrinkled rulers of the lineup gave us silent frowns that chilled the blood. I had the sense they never forgot, and, years later, one of them, beachboy Albert "Rabbit" Kekai, confirmed my hunch was true.

"I remember you," a man with brown skin, aquiline features and long, straight, sun-bleached hair called out to me one day in the lineup at Tongg's, staring at me poker-faced with big, reflective eyes that reminded me of glass fishermen's floats. "I'm Rabbit. I used to see you at Queens."

these majesties and unsure what, exactly, they meant.

"Eh, wake up already, you kids, Kekahili-Mindy-Nalani, whassamatta you! Turn your boards around and paddle, paddle hard," Shippy would shout in a booming voice and, startled, we would scramble to obey. Other times, if we got

I smiled and told him my name. Although he was coaching another girl that day, after she caught a wave he'd turn to me and give me critiques and tips and tell me when to go on waves. This continued, off and on, for years of chance encounters; Rabbit was a natural, generous teacher and young at heart.

But above and beyond the folks she knows, Cat said she also loves surfing because all its participants are, at heart, members of an oceangoing fellowship that can rely on one another when things get rough. Any surfer, "even the biggest jackass guy out there, will help you if you're in trouble," she said. It's a story all Hawai'i news reporters have filed, time and again: When first responders get a 911 call about an ocean emergency and rush to the site, they find surfers already administering CPR to the person they've pulled from the sea.

Cat was self-taught and started relatively late, in her twenties. Like most beginners on O'ahu, she first paddled out at Waikīkī. Elsewhere around the island, local kids begin wave riding at the nearest beach or at family friendly places with accessible, inside breaks such as Tongg's, White Plains in 'Ewa Beach, Mākaha Beach Park, Hale'iwa Ali'i Beach Park, Chun's Reef, Waimānalo Beach Park, and Kailua Beach Park. But Waikīkī, the storied break where George Freeth and Duke Kahanamoku is the piko (the navel) and the moe pai pai, the cradle, in the nursery of surfing.

ONCE SHE WAS ON THE WAVE SHE FORGOT HER FEAR IN THE THRILL AND JOY OF THE RIDE.

In Waikīkī, in the late 1950s, Laola Lake Aea's father, Thomas Lake, took her surfing for the first time. "In those days, there was a surf break alongside the Diamond Head wall of the Waikīkī Natatorium," said Laola, now an esthetician and ocean safety volunteer who lives and surfs on Kaua'i. "I was somewhere under five years old, and my dad paddled me out from Kaimana Beach on his redwood board."

Her first reaction, sensibly, was fear. "The whitewater looked so dangerous, and when my dad pushed me onto the wave I was screaming 'No! Too big! Too big!'" But there was no stopping, and once she was on the wave she forgot her fear in the thrill and joy of the ride. She demanded to be put on wave after wave, and in a few weeks she was paddling out on her own.

Laola, like many women, also loves surfing because it provided a healing outlet during a difficult time. When she was nine years old, as her parents were in the midst of getting a divorce, their house suddenly burned to the ground. Laola, her mother Lydia, and brothers Tommy, Russell, and Whitney, relocated to live full-time in Waikīkī.

"My mom worked at the Royal Hawaiian Hotel, which at the time had some cottages on the beach, and they told her, you just come live here," Laola re-

↑ Four generations of Hawaiian waterwomen: (left to right) Lydia Lake, Sanoe Lake-Eaton, Laola Lake Aea, Sage Eaton. Photo by River Eaton

calls. The children still saw their father, who worked in Waikīkī, playing Hawaiian music with his brother in the storied Kahauanu Lake Trio. She also studied hula with her aunt, legendary kumu hula Maiki Souza Aiu Lake, a key leader in the Hawaiian Renaissance of the late 1970s.

Laola and her brothers felt lucky to be living in a cottage right on Waikīkī Beach, overlooking three famous surf spots. "We surfed Canoes, Pops, and Number Threes. We surfed every single day, and then we would make tipis with our boards and sometimes sleep on the beach. Everything was so safe then."

Laola's daughter, Sanoe Lake Eaton, said her father put her on the front of his board when she was two years old. "I got my own board at five. Around ten years old, I really got into it, going out together with a girlfriend on the south side by the Beach House, at Po'ipū."

She grew up to become an accomplished shortboard surfer and a star of the film *Blue Crush,* which "was about women surfing, but also about friendship, that's one of my favorite things about surfing."

As far as why she loved surfing, it was hard to describe because "only a surfer knows the feeling," she said. "You can relate to other surf friends on a level that's different than with anybody else."

She described herself as typical. "Surfers tend to be solo rollers. Finding friends is nice, so you're not totally alone, but ultimately you're out there to catch a wave for yourself, to get the good, sweet ride with a big open face all to yourself."

A California resident, where she and her husband own a restaurant in the mountain ski resort of Big Bear, Sanoe wants her daughter and son to learn to surf but doesn't push it. "I want them to play and enjoy it, kind of like I did as a kid. I take them in summer down to the beach. They have little soft-topped boards and ride over a little sandbar that's forgiving." The family also returns frequently to Hawai'i.

One of Jyoti Mau's first teachers was Tiger Espere, a leading North Shore surfer from the 1960s and 70s, a close family friend who encouraged Jyoti, her two sisters, and her mother to surf. "So when Tiger came to town he'd take us out at Waikīkī, and he ended up making surfboards for us," Jyoti said. "He was very encouraging and supportive," added the adept longboarder, who handles the steep, fast waves of Suis with grace.

"And then at age fourteen, I just started going on my own at Queens, Canoes, and Pops with this little crew of girlfriends who I still am super good friends with," Jyoti added. The girl group eventually expanded their reach to Concessions,

↑ Press photo from *Blue Crush* featuring main characters Marie Chadwick (Kate Bosworth), Eden (Michelle Rodriguez) and Lena (Sanoe Lake). Universal Studios

Hawaiian surfer Sydney laukea surfs a wave at
Tavarua, Fiji. Photo by Scott Winer

which breaks offshore from Ala Moana Regional Park, "and when we'd get adventurous, we'd go to, like, Toes, in Niu Valley, on the East Side."

In her college years and "right before I became a mom," she had plenty of time to go surfing on her own. "I love surfing by myself," she says. "After I had the boys, if I could steal a moment here or there, I would."

In recent years, she's been able to surf with her husband, Keith, and their sons, "and I so love that we can share being in the ocean together," she says.

Surfing, Jyoti added, "is the perfect family everything, I feel."

From childhood, Maui native Sydney laukea was a childhood competitive swimmer and paddler as well as a model and beauty contest winner, but she didn't start surfing until her teens. "It was harder to get a surfboard back then," Sydney said, noting she and her sister were raised by a single mother who worked two jobs, and surfboards were expensive. She wanted to surf, however; her idols were older Maui waterwomen Laura and Carol Blears, sisters of 1972 world surfing champ Jimmy Blears, and daughters of James "Lord Talley-Ho" Blears, a celebrated professional wrestler and sports announcer. Sydney's father, the renowned pro wrestler "King" Curtis Iaukea, had been a football star and Waikīkī beachboy, and was a friend and protégé of Lord Blears. Laura Blears was a Makaha Invitational champion and one of the first Hawai'i women pro surfers.

Sydney finally started surfing in a class at Kamehameha Schools in Kapalama, O'ahu, after she became a boarding student there. "They took us to Waikīkī and we got to learn the right way, from the beachboys," she said. "Then after I graduated and went back to Maui, Ho'okipa is where I really learned to surf."

Ho'okipa, on Maui's north shore, is famous for its fierce winds and big, powerful winter waves and as an expert-only break dominated by local surfers. "A lot of guys I grew up with were really good, and it was exciting to see them ripping," she said. "It was literally all boys, except for a little group of girls at Ho'okipa, a real community of five or six of us, including Lynn Blomfield, who became the mother of Honolua Blomfield (a longboard world champion) and Annie Kinoshita, who's married to Matt Kinoshita (the owner of Kazuma Surfboards on Maui, who runs a surf coaching program for local kids)."

Having learned to hold her own with her female friends in a male world at Ho'okipa, Sydney is able to keep her composure and get waves at competitive O'ahu lineups from the North Shore to Ala Moana Bowls, as well as the powerful, big-wave break at Ricebowls on the South Shore, "where I'm usually the only girl."

Sydney Iaukea fits her board into her truck. Photo by Dennis Oda

Debbie Millikan at Suis. Photo by Dennis Oda

Sydney said he'e nalu is a nice way to connect with other people. Even if she doesn't run into friends, she still enjoys the lineup social scene. "I kinda like it because it is so mundane, so low-impact on brain capacity," she said. "It's a different way to connect to people who we don't even know their occupations, as well as with the friends we've had out here for decades. It's special."

As our Suis pal, bartender Peter Ono, aka "Boogie Pete," said recently, "I never felt I missed out on social life during the pandemic."

On an intellectual, spiritual, and emotional level, Sydney also connects with her Hawaiian heritage through surfing. "I learned aloha kai (ocean) is part of it, it's not just aloha 'āina (land), for in Hawaiian epistemology, 'āina flows into kai and every part of (nature) has a name, for instance, every wind."

But the prime joy of surfing, for Sydney, is feeling at one with nature. After sitting out at sea in a lineup such as Suis, for so many years, "you can tell what's happening out there; you have a different lens and you know where the current is flowing, what the wind, waves, honu, and birds are doing," she said. "One time a seabird came straight for me and we literally shared the wave, and it felt like confirmation I'm on the right track."

Debbie Millikan concurs. "To me, it's about the experience of being in nature, feeling that connection with Mother Ocean," said the educator and mother of two. "It's just home, where I should be."

"Surfing for me is the place where you can reset everything, totally at peace in the ocean, away from work and family, and the so many things in life you're supposed to be doing, tending to, stressful things," said Kiana Blankenfeld, a Kailua fitness trainer, gym manager, and mother of two. "It's where you can be in nature and be by yourself."

WE HAWAIIANS USED TO CLEANSE OURSELVES IN THE WATER WHEN WE WERE SICK. FOR ME, IT'S DEFINITELY SELF-CARE TO GO OUT, WORK MY BODY AND BE IN THE MOMENT, LEAVE MY TROUBLES ON THE SAND.

– MAY KAMAKA

Blankenfeld sometimes gives surf lessons to neophytes who want to join Surfing Moms, which requires that members have taken enough surfing lessons to know basic skills and water safety rules.

May Kamaka said she's Native Hawaiian on both sides and wanted to learn surfing, but no one in her nuclear family surfed and she was afraid of the ocean. She got over her fear after her mother enrolled her in a kids' surfing program overseen by the beachboys at Waikīkī.

"Surfing to me is like an escape, like music," said May, a member of the family that founded Kamaka Ukulele. "We Hawaiians used to cleanse ourselves in the water when we were sick. For me, it's definitely self-care to go out, work my body and be in the moment, leave my troubles on the sand."

"Paddling out, I feel I'm releasing emotions, freeing myself," said May's friend, Izzie Cleofe. "Paddling and riding a wave, I can let out anger and aggression—it helps my surfing and doesn't hurt anybody."

Before their interviews, Izzie, May, and her friends had tried Suis, a new spot for them, and Izzie said she had felt nervous until she confided her fears to Debbie Millikan and Melissa Kurpinski, older and more experienced surfers who told her they felt nervous, too. Then Debbie, an expert surfer, gave all of them some tips about Suis, her home break.

"Riding a wave feels honestly empowering. I can give myself more positive self-talk, telling myself look, with all the fear you have, you're doing this," Izzie said. One of the biggest lessons she's learned from surfing, she added, was that her worst fear was not having control of everything around her, but when she entered the water she realized she was surrendering herself to it, and it felt good.

"My dad used to just know," Ane Bakutis said. "He'd say, 'You're grouchy. You need to get in the water.'" She'd paddle out at Mākaha and feel better as soon as she got offshore.

↑↓ Early morning surf session at Suis. Veteran surfers Kim Heyer and Melissa Kurpinski gives some pointers to younger surfers (left to right) May Kamaka, Wendy Sakuma, Isabel "Izzie" Cleofe, and Mikayla Brennan before they go off to surf Suis for the first time. Photos by Dennis Oda

→ The Westside Wahines. Photo courtesy Kathy Terada

→ Kathy Terada tandem surfs with Brian Keaulana. Photo by Don King

Surfing, for Ane, is "an essential connection to the source and back to nature that heals you physically and spiritually, takes away any stress or heartache. I get real peace and tranquility."

And, she added, the connection with nature is augmented by a connection to the Hawaiian past and people she surfed with who are no longer living, especially Rell Sunn and Pua Mokuau.

Kathy Terada, one of the original Westside Wahines, misses Sunn and Mokuau every day. "They were my hula sisters," she said. She feels their presence in the water and also in her work supporting community and women's health. For forty-five years, she has been a nurse-practitioner at Waianae Comprehensive Health Center and a resident of Mākaha, where she and her husband raised their two sons.

A swimmer and bodyboarder, Kathy was inspired to learn surfing by the Sunn sisters, who folded her into their charmed circle of friends, including the Bakutis and Keaulana families. She also learned tandem surfing as the partner of John DeSoto and Brian Keaulana, with whom she competed until recently in contests around the world.

"I used to help Rell with her menehune surf contests," Kathy said. "She

← ↑ Young surfers compete in Duane DeSoto's Menehune Contest in 2021, Mākaha.
Photos by Ha'a Keaulana

99

Young surfer competing in Duane DeSoto's Menehune Contest in 2021, Mākaha. Photo by Haʻa Keaulana

was so, so special; there'll never be another person like her. She wanted to teach kids about the ocean, give them a healthy, safe place to be."

At the contests and as a teacher, "she was so encouraging—she made everything fun. She knew all the kids, and when she would announce the contestants, she would tell you stories about each child, and great surfers grew out of her contests."

Sunn also taught children how to dive and spearfish on the reef, and "whatever she caught she would cook and invite everybody over to eat."

With a laugh, Kathy said Sunn got so excited out surfing she couldn't help herself; she'd abandon etiquette to the winds. "She would tell me go, and then she would just cut me off." But because of Sunn's charm and generosity in everything else, she was instantly forgiven.

She speaks of Sunn at times in the present tense, as if she's still alive. "Mostly I liked to just watch her surf, so beautiful, effortless. She catches a wave by reflex, and she's in the peak, it just picks her up. Always laughing, she's the best storyteller. If you're around her, you can't help but love surfing and want to surf."

With age, Kathy has become a bit more careful out surfing, but she feels confident because "the regulars watch out for us and make sure we're safe."

Instead of venturing out to the bigger waves she used to enjoy with the Westside Wahines, Kathy now surfs the inside, keiki break with groups of young girls who look up to her as a mentor. She helps and comforts them when they say they feel afraid as bigger sets roll in. But next thing she knows, they're paddling out to meet those waves, while she finds herself surrounded by the next new crop of little girls. She wouldn't have it any other way. And, "now that I'm so much older, I hear young kids always saying, 'Go auntie go!'" She laughed. "And they comment on your wave. Yeah, it's a happy place."

Like Kathy Terada, Jennifer Lee Van Gieson was welcomed and recruited to Mākaha by Sunn. Jenn grew up in town, surfing her home break of Waikīkī, but when she was eight years old she entered one of Sunn's first menehune contests. One of the only two girls who participated at the time, she was hānai'ed, adopted, as a protegé by Sunn, who often invited to her to stay at her home. "She would leave me messages, tell me how the waves were and to come out for the weekend," Jenn said.

"There was another girl, Melanie Bartel—I was a longboarder, she was an all-boarder. We were in the first group Aunty Rell took to compete at the surf festival Biarritiz, France, and we also made a holoholo trip to check out Spain. Before, for us Hawai'i kids to go to another country was not even on the radar, we were just stoked to go to another island."

At Biarritz, the Mākaha natives danced a hula as part of a cultural exchange. "It definitely gave me a different perspective on life at a really young age; I was like thirteen. It broadened my horizons for sure. Back then in Hawai'i, we weren't really taught about the big world out there." Jenn studied about different countries and traveled as a competitive stand-up surfer to the British Virgin Islands, China, Hong Kong, and Tahiti.

"I owe it to Rell. The people I met, the way she taught me to be as a person, taught me to bridge a lot of gaps and make relationships I wouldn't

↑ Rell Sunn demonstrating power and grace, 1979. Photo by Ken Sakamoto/Honolulu Star-Bulletin have if wasn't for her. She made every kid feel like they were the most special child in the world," Jenn said. "And she was so young at heart, it made her feel more youthful being around kids, and I feel like it took her mind off her illness as well."

Sunn died in 1997, but to this day, "I feel when I'm surfing, I'm surfing with Aunty Rell, and other uncles and aunties I've lost. I feel like they're there," Jenn said. "Surfing is very spiritual. When my life gets super hectic, the ocean is the place I go to for release, to feel that connection with the past," she said. "Like, it's going to be okay. All that stuff on land, that's small."

> THE OCEAN IS THE PLACE I GO TO FOR RELEASE, TO FEEL THAT CONNECTION WHERE I'M BACKED BY THOSE PEOPLE IN THE PAST, LIKE, IT'S GOING TO BE OKAY. ALL THAT STUFF ON LAND, THAT'S SMALL.
>
> — JENNIFER GIESON

Others who first took off in Waikīkī include three Black surfer-influencers from the mainland. "When I moved to Hawai'i, I started accepting myself and feeling confident in my own skin," Dominique "Nique" Miller told the surf website The Inertia in 2022. "On the mainland, especially (in 2011), it wasn't cool to look like me—dark skin, crazy hair, broader features, and a more athletic build," she said, praising the diversity and inclusiveness she found here. Respectful and friendly to locals, Miller was quickly adopted by the regulars at Queens and progressed quickly, qualifying for the longboard and SUP world tours in 2014 and becoming sponsored by Billabong.

Fellow Waikīkī alumna Rhonda Harper cofounded Black Girls Surf, a nonprofit that conducts surf camps for local girls and women in Africa, the Caribbean, and the U.S. Her colleague, Whittney-Anela Soares, leads remote training sessions from her home on the Big Island, where she grew up and lives with her family and hopes to establish the first Black Girls Surf camp in Hawai'i. "It's very 'ohana-oriented here," Soares told *Hawaii Business Magazine* in 2020, adding for wahine, that's a big plus.

Honolulu native Kai'ulu Downing also got her start at Waikīkī. Her father, George Downing, was a pioneer big-wave rider, a Waikīkī beachboy, surfboard manufacturer, and the man who decided whether the waves were big and good enough to hold the Quiksilver in Honor of Eddie Aikau Big Wave Invitational at Waimea Bay. In 1990, her older brother, Keone Downing, won the "Eddie," which as of 2022 had only been held nine times since 1984. A jewelry and apparel designer,

Kai'ulu works alongside Keone at Downing Hawaii, the family surf shop in Kaimukī.

Her favorite spot is Queen's in Waikīkī. The long, steep, feathering waves break in both directions, but it is the right-peeling wave on which a regular-foot surfer like Kai'ulu rides left foot forward, facing the wall, that is revered.

Kai'ulu's father and mother, Gildea Lawae Downing, ran the Waikiki Beach Center when she, Keone, and their brother Kainoa were children. Like many island girls, Kai'ulu was taught to surf by her father. She and George were surfing together at Queen's when, at age thirteen, she rode the most memorable wave of her life. "It was five feet (by Hawaiian measure, a wave with a 10-foot face), the biggest wave I ever caught," she said.

"I never liked big waves, but my dad told me to paddle. I didn't look, I just paddled and I made the wave," she remembered with a proud smile.

"Once I got out there, I always felt the water was so healing," Kai'ulu said, adding she hadn't surfed much in years. She was busy helping and later caring for her parents, but she still paddled outrigger canoe until the Covid pandemic struck and she took up pickleball.

Which is fine, one senses. The ocean is always there, and that one perfect wave will last forever.

Surfing lesson, 1983. Honolulu Star-Bulletin

↑ Pre-Waimea paddle out for Women of the Bay opening ceremony, with Paige Alms, Keala Kennelly, and Raquel Heckert. Photo by Betty Depolito

# EARLY TWENTIETH CENTURY

Women were surfing with skill and commitment as early as the 1910s at Waikīkī. Sisters Marion Elizabeth "Babe" Keohoku'ilanikauleleaiwi and Beatrice Puaikalani Dowsett were famed for being the first to ride tandem in a threesome on one board along with Duke Kahanamoku. Josephine Pratt and Mildred Turner were the first female members of Hui Nalu, Waikīkī's original surf and canoe club, founded in 1908 at the Moana Hotel by Kahanamoku, Knute Cottrell, and Ken Winter. Other admired early twentieth century surfers included Leslie Lemon, Beatrice Newport, Cecily Cunha, Marchien Wehselau, Dot Hammond, and Babe Gillespie.

## MID-CENTURY

In the 1940s, by most accounts, the leading Hawai'i female surfer was Keanuenue Kaeo Rochlen. And veteran oceangoers reminisce about Mary Ann Hawkins, a California swimming champion and pioneer board surfer who moved to Hawai'i and founded a swimming school for young children. Hawkins further distinguished herself as a bodysurfer, able to steer herself across the face of the wave and perform maneuvers using her body as if it were a board.

During the postwar boom, women surfers got a chance to show their mettle in the first world surfing championships, held at Mākaha Beach. The Makaha International Surfing Contest, sponsored by the Waikiki Surf Club, was launched as a men's-only event in the winter, big-wave season of 1954, but added a women's division in 1956.

In 1956, Ethel Kukea, a Californian who married a Hawaiian surfer, was crowned the first women's Mākaha champion. The runner-up was Betty Pembroke Heldreich, another Californian, who had started surfing at age forty-one in Waikīkī. After she and her husband divorced, Betty moved to a beachfront property at Mākaha. "My dad was not the most pleasant guy to be around, and Mother definitely gained her strength and courage to leave him through surfing," said her eldest daughter Vicky Heldreich Durand, author of *Wave Woman: The Life and Struggles of a Surfing Pioneer,* a captivating memoir of her mother and life on O'ahu's West Side.

"A lot of girls surf, but how many mothers at age forty, fifty, or sixty would have that spirit of adventure? I was really lucky that

TRAILBLAZERS

104

Mother brought me into surfing," Vicky said.

In 1957, Betty Heldreich won the International Surfing Meet at Lima, Peru; later that year, seventeen-year-old Vicky was crowned Mākaha women's champ.

Californian Marge Calhoun won the Mākaha championship in 1958. When she died in 2017, her obituary erroneously called her the first women's Mākaha champion. She was actually the third, behind Ethel Kukea and Vicky.

"We were forgotten," Vicky said. "That's why I wrote my book."

In Mākaha, people don't forget. Bunky Bakutis and Buffalo Keaulana speak with admiration and affection of Betty and Vicky. And Betty made another lifetime friend when she lost her board and swam in to find a seven-year-old girl playing with it in the shorebreak. The little girl was Rell Sunn. Forty years later, a month before Rell died of breast cancer at age forty-seven, she paid a call on eighty-four-year-old Betty. They talked surfing.

## 1959–1960s

In a decade defined by youth, counterculture, and protest, wom-

en's surfing took off worldwide. Californian, Linda Benson, winner of the 1959 Mākaha contest, went on to place first in the first West Coast Surf Championship held at Huntington Beach. Throughout the sixties, Benson traded wins in state, regional, and national competitions with California's Joyce Hoffman and Hawai'i's Joey Hamasaki. Following in Joey's footsteps, Rell Sunn won the Hawai'i junior women's state championship in 1965, and in 1966, competed in the world championships at Huntington Beach, California, on a team of island teens chaperoned by Duke Kahanamoku.

Despite the preeminence of the Makaha Championship, Hawai'i was displaced by Australia as the birthplace of the first world surfing contest. The International Surfing Federation, the promoter of amateur surf events (now the International Surfing Association), announced the first official world contest was its event in 1964 at Australia's Manly Beach.

Mākaha's demotion to first "unofficial" world title event was indicative of how westerners were appropriating the sport that had been introduced to California in 1885 by Hawaiian princes David Kawananakoa, Edward Keli'iahonui, and Jonah Kūhiō Kalaniana'ole, and in the early twentieth century by George Freeth and

# The Purist

Throughout the 1960s, Joey Hamasaki, the first Hawai'i native and Asian American woman to become a professional surfer, won or placed second in several prestigious contests and had a Wardy surfboard model named for her. She quit surfing early on due to hip injuries and died in 2022, largely overlooked by surf media and unknown to the generations of island surfers that followed her.

At sixteen, Joey won the 1962 Hawai'i state junior women's championship and left the islands for Southern California. "Joey was one of the first to take 'local-style' wahine surfing to the mainland and become a force to be reckoned with," Gerry Lopez said. She won the 1965 Western Regional Surfing Championships, the 1966 Malibu Invitational, and the 1967 U.S. East Coast Surfing Championships. She placed second behind Joyce Hoffman in the 1964 Makaha International and the 1966 World Championships in the U.S. Surfing Association final ratings and Surfer Poll Awards in 1965 and 1967.

Joey rode for Hobie, Jacobs, Weber and Wardy Surfboards, and was recruited as a member of the Windandsea pro surf team; she traveled to surf in Australia, New Zealand, Fiji, and Tahiti, coming home every winter to spend Christmas in Honolulu with her family and compete in the Makaha International Contest. Often she stayed with Rell Sunn and her sisters, including Mākaha champion Martha Sunn.

"Without even trying to be, she became an ambassador of aloha in the tradition of the Duke," Lopez said. "Joey-girl took her aloha to the mainland where they never have enough...that's where it was needed and maybe that's where it blossomed for her."

↑ Joey Hamasaki. Photo by LeRoy Gannis

Duke Kahanamoku. The Duke had also brought surfing to Australia whose citizens went wild for the sport and soon became top international contenders.

In 1959, Benson, at age fifteen, was also proclaimed the first female to ride big waves at Waimea Bay, soon after Greg Noll, Pat Curren, and other Californians were recognized as the first-ever big Waimea riders in 1957. While admiring their brave achievements, some of us born and raised in the islands are skeptical to hear mainlanders lauded as the first riders of Waimea. The environs of the bay—the enormous river valley filled with agricultural terraces, crowned by waterfalls and a great heiau overlooking the sea; the fisheries off the long, broad white sand beach bracketed by lava rock cliffs—supported a teeming population in pre-contact days. Before westerners arrived in Hawai'i, surfing had been practiced and witnessed for hundreds of years by the indigenous people who invented it.

Karin Amimoto Ingersoll, author of a cultural history of he'e nalu in the islands, says it's likely that Hawaiians, male and female, rode big Waimea as well as Sunset Beach and other North Shore breaks. Even much more recently, "As Rabbit (Keikai) has explained, several Hawaiian surfers, including many from Waikīkī, often rode North Shore waves at places like Pau Malu (Sunset Beach), Pipeline, and even Waimea Bay in the 1940s," Isaiah Helekunihi Walker writes in *Waves of Resistance: Surfing and History in Twentieth-Century Hawaii*, citing an interview with the late Waikīkī beachboy Albert "Rabbit" Kekai. Walker, an assistant professor of history at Brigham Young University-Hawai'i, adds that in the late fifties and early sixties, Hawaiians also surfed big North Shore waves, including the young Kealoha Kaio, recognized by locals "as the first to make a hard bottom-turn at Waimea Bay."

But the glamorous images of haole surfers in Hawaiian waves, playing to a prosperous target audience, were central to the commercialization of surfing in the sixties. Ironically, just as the sport solidified as a mainstream lifestyle trend and more women surfed competitively, they began losing opportunities to men. Now that there was good money to be made through sponsorships and product endorsements for everything from surfboards and equipment to apparel and cars, surfer guys pushed the girls aside to grab the limelight, fortune, and fame. The backwash had begun.

# The Lawyer

In the 1970s, Evelyn "Evie" Black won the Hawaiʻi state championship three times and was crowned U.S. women's surfing champion. "In those days, to win (the U.S. championship) at Huntington Beach, you had to shoot the pier, and I could see the big, sharp barnacles close-up as I rode between the pilings, so I knew I could not fall off," she said.

Her goal was to be a pro surfer, but in her senior year at Punahou School, her grandfather offered some advice. "He told me, 'You can be a beach bum, or you can go to college and do something with your life.'" Taking his advice, she attended the University of Southern California.

Returning home after graduation, she worked as a surfing stunt double for Cheryl Ladd on *Charlie's Angels* while the they filmed an episode titled "Angels in Paradise." "We were shooting at the Royal Hawaiian, and they had hired off-duty police for security. One of the officers, Timmy Wong, became my husband."

Evie became an HPD officer for two years, then earned her J.D. from the University of Santa Clara law school in California. She returned to practice maritime and admiralty law in Honolulu. Now retired and a widow after forty-two years of marriage, she still gets in the water with Kaiʻulu Downing, her first surfing buddy and lifelong friend.

↑ Evie Black and her surfing coach, Rabbit Kekai, hold their respective trophies for the Hawaiʻi State Surfing Championship when Black won the women's division in the 1970s. Photo courtesy Evie Black

## 1970s–1980s

Pro surfing debuted in the early seventies, with men receiving sponsorship support and remunerative prize purses, while women "traveled all over the world to compete, spending their own money" for the chance to win paltry amounts, said Laola Lake-Aea, who surfed competitively for a time.

The group included Rell Sunn, who had returned home to raise her baby daughter after a sojourn on the mainland. In 1977, she was hired as the first female lifeguard at Mākaha Beach.

In addition to big names such as California champion Jericho Poppler, seventies Hawai'i stars included three-time state champion Becky Benson; her sister Blanche, a tandem champion and known for surfing big Sunset Beach; and Laura Lee Ching, formerly Laura Blears.

In 1973, Laura was invited to be the first woman to compete against the men in the Smirnoff Pro Am World Championship at Sunset Beach. The Smirnoff had been an all-male event since its debut in 1969, when Margo Godfrey won the women's division. Laura, who had won the 1972 Makaha International, didn't win the Smirnoff, but she did gain an advertising contract and

appeared on television game and sports shows, as well as in *Playboy* magazine, which featured her surfing in the nude. The Smirnoff Pro Am reinstated a women's division in its 1976 and 1977 events, both won by Jericho Poppler.

In 1975, Poppler, Mary Lou Drummy, Linda Westfall, and others co-founded the Women's International Surfing Association (WISA) in California and began raising sponsor money and launching a women's world tour.

Also in 1975, the nonprofit Hawaii Women's Surfing Hui was co-founded on O'ahu's North Shore by Rell Sunn, Laola Lake-Aea, Jeannie Chesser, Patti Paniccia, and others, "to get our own sponsors, our own contests," Laola said. "In 1976 we put on the first all-women's, pro surf contest at Haleiwa."

The International Professional Surfers (IPS) world pro circuit, founded in 1976 by 1968 world champion Fred Hemmings and Randy Rarick, held contests in Hawai'i, Australia, Brazil, and South Africa. Because they had to pay their own way, only six women— Becky Benson, Claudia Kravitz, Patti Paniccia Jericho Poppler, Sally Prange, and Rell Sunn made it to the kickoff event in Durban, South Africa. Ultimately, due to discrepancies and unfairness on the women's tour such as inade-

# The Environmentalist

In the mid-1980s, when Debbie Millikan was in middle school in Huntington Beach, California, she noticed there weren't many other girls her age out surfing and the older women weren't riding shortboards like her. "I don't think I ever saw a woman actually surfing a wave other than 'Gidget' style, standing on a longboard in a bikini," Debbie said. "They were gliding, but not ripping."

Title IX made a positive difference in Debbie's surfing life. In her junior year of high school, Debbie transferred to Mater Dei, a private school in Santa Ana and joined their all-male surf team. "I was the only girl, surfing against boys," she said. Because of Title IX, they had to take her.

In college, Debbie took a semester off to travel with her boyfriend, a pro surfer on the world championship tour. The couple's plan was to surf new breaks and learn about different cultures together. Instead, she found herself shooting videos of his heats and jotting down his scores. Sometimes she would get in the water as his caddy, paddling out on a spare surfboard and waiting just outside the competition zone in case his board got damaged and he needed to swap.

"I quickly realized it was all about him," she said. "'What am I doing?' I thought." She'd paid for a surf trip but she wasn't surfing.

Enough, she decided. She would try out for the women's division and focus on her own surfing. From then on, wherever they traveled, Debbie would surf qualifying heats and pay the fee to enter women's events. After a few itinerant semesters, she stopped competing to focus on academics, but the experience upped her game for life and she had a lot more fun than just being a tourist and spectator.

↑ Debbie Millikan surfing Suis. Photo by Dennis Oda

quate prize money at some stops, no women's world champion was named that year.

In 1977, IPS revisited its women's tour and began out-competing WISA for sponsor funding. Answering back, the women formed the Women's Professional Surfing Association (WPS) in 1979. But IPS won the battle, monopolizing professional surfing for both genders. It became the Association of Surfing Professionals (ASP) in 1983 and has been the World Surf League (WSL) since 2015.

The seventies and eighties were excellent decades for Hawai'i women. "I recall being astonished by the Hawaiian women when they came out for pro events, just thinking what powerful people they appeared," Nick Carroll,

a renowned Australian surfer of the era, reminisced to surf writer Alicia King in 2018.

O'ahu's Lynne Boyer won the world championship in 1978 and 1979, and Kaua'i's Margo Oberg took the world titles in 1975, 1977, 1980, 1981, and 1983.

## 1980s

In the eighties and early nineties, Australia's Jodie Cooper and Hawai'i's Rell Sunn were transformative influencers. Cooper won thirteen events on the women's world tour and blazed through barrels at Backdoor Pipeline in the eighties. She was also one of the first female pro surfers to come out as gay.

TRAILBLAZERS

← Stephanie Gilmore surfing in the Quarter Finals of the Womens Hawaiian Pro at Hale'iwa in 2010 Triple Crown of Surfing

# The Barreler

Ranked in the top ten of world championship contestants throughout the 1990s, Rochelle Ballard of Kaua'i never won a world title, but she's ranked first in surfing history as the defining female barrel rider at Banzai Pipeline. There weren't any women's competitions at the dangerous break at the time, so learning to excel—and survive—at Pipeline and Backdoor was a personal goal with no material rewards in sight.

When she moved to O'ahu's North Shore in 1995, friends pointed her towards Pipeline and "were like, 'go out and just pull in, because not many girls are getting barrelled and getting out,'" she said.

Persistence and guts began to win her respect and space in the lineup. "I learned to drop in late from the boys, and I started getting better barrels and coming out."

In 1997, at the Billabong Pro at Burleigh Heads, Australia, Rochelle scored two perfect ten barrel rides against Layne Beachley in the semifinals and went on to win the event over Lisa Andersen and be ranked second in the world that year. She still holds the women's world record for scoring two perfect tens (receiving a ten from each judge on the panel) in a single heat.

Rochelle and her husband at the time, filmmaker Bill Ballard, set out to show the world how females were really surfing. With Megan Abubo, Keala Kennelley, Layne Beachley, Serena Brooke, Kate Skarratt, and other friends, they traveled to find and surf beautiful, high-caliber waves. Bill filmed their rides and the fun adventure and sisterly solidarity of their lifestyle.

Their 1998 video "Blue Crush," which included Pipeline footage, proved such a hit that a Hollywood production team bought the rights to the title and made the 2002 feature film of the same name, with Bill as a consultant and Rochelle, and her comrades in the cast.

After retiring from the pros, Rochelle led wellness retreats and founded Surf Into Yoga, for which she teaches yoga and surfing classes. "And I still surf my brains out whenever I can," and it's all free surfing, she said.

→ Rochelle Ballard at Backdoor. Photo by Tony Heff

In 1982, Sunn was ranked number one in the world for women's longboard surfing. In 1983, she was among the first five women inducted into the International Surfing Museum's Walk of Fame in Huntington Beach, California. Despite being diagnosed with recurring breast cancer over the years, she pursued her dreams, competing around the world, and holding her annual Menehune Contest for keiki in Mākaha.

Other late eighties–early nineties phenoms included world champions Wendy Botha, Frieda Zamba, Pam Burridge, and Pauline Menczer.

## 1990s

Californian Lisa Andersen won the world championship four times in the 1990s, while Layne Beachley continued accumulating world titles well into the aughts, seven in all, a record that stood until 2018 when it was matched by her countrywoman, Stephanie Gilmore, and then surpassed in 2022 when Gilmore won her eighth world title.

In 1997, a women's division was added to the Vans Triple Crown of Surfing on O'ahu's North Shore, although the women only competed at Hale'iwa and Sunset Beach. Although women had surfed Pipeline since four-time U.S. champion Joyce Hoffman led the way in 1968, the Pipeline segment of the Crown remained exclusive to the men. Beachley won the inaugural championship and again in 1998. Hawai'i winners included the famously daring Keala

# TRAILBLAZERS

↑ Betty Depolito on a wave at Sunset Beach in 1980. Photo by Jeff Divine

Kennelly who won four championship tour events at Teahupo'o, Tahiti, before the women's contest was canceled because the break was deemed too dangerous for them. After sixteen years, the women's Tahiti event returned in 2022 alongside the men's.

Other Hawai'i stars of the nineties were O'ahu surfer Megan Abubo and Kaua'i's Rochelle Ballard, both of whom also won several events on the world championship tour.

Ballard is famous for her incomparable, hard-won mastery of Banzai Pipeline. Competing with men for waves in the crowded lineup, Rochelle became celebrated as the best female barrel rider in the world. Her fellow North Shore resident "Banzai" Betty Depolito,

another Pipeline pioneer, held the first women's bodyboard contest at the barreling break in 1990 and put on the T&C Pipeline Championships for women in 2005. The shortboarding event was won by fifteen-year-old Alana Blanchard of Kaua'i.

## 2000s

The new millennium has brought groundbreaking advances for gender equity in women's pro surfing, although with one major setback: the women's Vans Triple Crown was canceled in 2011 due to lack of sponsorship funds. That year, Carissa Moore accepted the invitation to compete as the only woman in the Hale'iwa and Sunset Beach events. "If there were events for the girls, I wouldn't be surfing in the guys' events," the

114

eighteen-year-old said in an interview. She added she had just won her first world title, "but I won it away from home and would love to have finished it here." In 2011, the world tours had twelve men's events and seven for women, none in Hawai'i.

Still, upswings have outnumbered downturns so far.

In 2005, to the cheers of the surfing community, big-wave world champion Keala Kennelly came out as gay, followed a decade later by two-time world shortboard champion Tyler Wright. Longboard world champion Cori Schumacher and U.S. women's amateur longboard champion Sheri Crummer have also announced their LGBTQ status. Schumacher and Crummer founded "The History of Women's Surfing," an online archive. Keala and Tyler are candid, eloquent spokeswomen for inclusivity and being true to yourself in sports and life.

Further millennial milestones include the first women's big-wave competitions; the awarding of equal prize purses to men and women; and establishing an equal number of events for women and men with both genders competing during the same holding period at the same breaks.

Spearheading these changes were the Committee for Equity in Women's Surfing, co-founded by Sabrina Brennan, a commissioner with the San Mateo

← Tyler Wright Surfing in the Quarter final of the Hawaiian Pro Surf Contest at the 2010 Triple Crown of Surfing.

County Harbor District; California labor lawyer Karen Tynan; and big-wave surfers Andrea Moller, Keala Kennelly, and Paige Alms of Hawai'i, and Bianca Valenti of California. In Hawai'i, they joined intrepid equality advocates Betty Depolito, Wrenna Delgado, Jenn Marr, and Carol Philips to equalize the legislative landscape for surf contest permitting.

## EQUAL PAY

WSL began paying equal money in prize purses to women and men in 2019. Until then, the men earned nearly twice as much, as Ferd Lewis pointed out in his *Honolulu*

*Star-Advertiser* column in 2018. "When Carissa Moore of Hawaii won the Pro France surfing event she received a $60,000 check. Meanwhile, her male counterpart, Gabriel Medina of Brazil, cashed one for $100,000," Ferd wrote. "Same place and same dates, but vastly different paychecks."

"It is more than just prize money," Carissa told Ferd. "It was a huge statement (of) what it represents to be respected as an elite athlete on the same level as the men."

## BIG-WAVE WOMEN

The first women's big-wave event, called an "exhibition" rather than a contest because it offered no prize money, was held in 2000

↑ Keala Kennelly at Jaws. Photo by Richard Hallman, courtesy of Keala Kennelly

116

alongside a longtime men's event, the Nelscott Reef Big Wave Classic, at a forbidding cold mountain of a wave breaking a half-mile off the Oregon coast in waters laced with kelp and great white sharks. Keala Kennelly won. After a gap, eight women surfed in a "women's superheat" won by Bianca Valenti, again with no prize money offered, although the men's division ended up splitting its purse with the women. In 2019, Hawai'i's Emi Erickson won a full-on women's Nelscott Reef event where women finally received equal prize money to men.

At the big-wave spot called Maverick's, off Half Moon Bay State Beach in San Mateo, California, twenty-four men were invited to compete in an annual contest, no women allowed. In 2017, when the contest permit came up for renewal before the California Coastal Commission, the surf equity committee demanded that twelve women and twelve men be invited. The commission approved the permit for one year only, stipulating that renewal would depend on presentation of a plan to include women, but as of 2022 the Maverick's event had not been held since 2016.

Meanwhile, at Pe'ahi ("Jaws") in 2015, Maui native Paige Alms became the first woman to get barreled at the toothy break and won a WSL big wave award. Alms won the first women's Pe'ahi Challenge in 2016, which was also the debut event on the newly founded WSL women's big-wave tour. Alms won

← Carissa Moore surfing Kewalos. Photo by Craig T. Kojima/Honolulu Star-Advertiser

again in 2017 and 2019, while Kennelly took first place in 2018 .

That was also the year Betty Depolito, fellow North Shore surfer Wrenna Delgado, Polly Ralda, and others founded Queen of the Bay, a one-day, big-wave, invitational contest at Waimea Bay. As of the winter of 2022–2023, the event had never run due to the pandemic, lack of waves that met the threshold height of twenty feet Hawaiian, and no sponsors. Since 1986, the prime period for big waves at Waimea Bay, December through February, has traditionally been reserved for the one-day, Eddie Aikau Big-Wave Invitational.

Invitees were all male until 2016-2017, when a single woman, Keala Kennelly, was listed as an alternate and didn't surf. By 2022-2023, a total of fifty-two invitees included twelve women—six contestants and six alternates.

On January 22, 2023, the Eddie was called on for only the tenth time in its history, and with women competing in it for the first time alongside the men, surf history was made.

Meanwhile, Betty Depolito has kept advancing women's-only, big-wave events. In winter of 2020–2021, Betty canceled Women of the Bay due to the Covid pandemic, but launched

Red Bull Magnitude, a women's-only, big-wave contest held remotely, without in-person heats or audiences, at Pe'ahi, Waimea Bay and the Pipeline outer reefs. Over the several-weeks holding period, contestants received Red Bull-provided film and safety crews for free surf sessions; they submitted video of their top two waves to be judged. Hawai'i athletes swept the first Magnitude: Keala Kennelly in first place, Makani Adric in second, and Waimea Bay specialist Emi Erickson awarded best ride. The second year, Maui's Skylar Lickle won first place, Portugal's Michaela Fregonese (age thirty-eight) placed second, and Paige Alms won best ride. Other leading big wave surfers include Hawai'i's Andrea Moller and Kelta O'Rourke, California's Katie McConnell, Brazil's Raquel Heckert and Silvia Nabuco, Guatamala's Polly Ralda, Mexico's Isabelle Leonhardt, and Laura Enever of Australia.

As of 2022, there were three big wave events fielding men and women: WSL's TUDOR Nazaré and Quiksilver Jaws challenges and the Red Bull Big Wave Awards.

For years, Betty, Keala, and veteran North Shore surfers Jenn Marr and Carol Philips petitioned the Honolulu City Council and Department of Parks and Recreation, demanding that permitting rules for shorewater events be revised by requiring gender equity in competitions held at beach parks. In 2020, they won the passage of Resolution 20-12, known as the "surf equity resolution," and Bill 93, which mandates gender equity for all sports activities requiring a city park use permit.

Without waiting for the next permitting round, World Surf League announced it would include women's and men's divisions at all its events, to be held at the same surf breaks, starting with the 2022 world championship tour. The kickoff events for the tour would be the Billabong Pro Pipeline and Hurley Pro Sunset Beach.

In 2022, the Honolulu Department of Parks & Recreation proposed revisions to its permitting rules, strengthening its criteria for gender equity.

For women surfers, 2021, 2022 and 2023 were breakout years, marked by the 2021 debut of surfing as an Olympic sport; the return of a women's Vans Triple Crown and the debut of WSL women's championship tour events on Oʻahu's North Shore; and women competing in the Eddie Aikau Invitational for the first time.

TRAILBLAZERS

Oʻahu surfer Joy Monahan, 2008 women's longboard world champion surfing on a longboard in Waikīkī.

Hawai'i's Carissa Moore won Olympic surfing gold in 2021 and placed first in the Vans Triple Crown in 2021, 2022 (when she swept all three contests) ,and 2023 (when she won the Sunset event and highest total points against Moana Jones Wong, who won at Pipeline, and Zoe McDougall, who won at Hale'iwa).

In January 2022, women participated for the first time in the Da Hui Backdoor Shootout, an annual, invitation-only competition at Pipeline. "Women have always been invited, but they lacked sponsors to pay the entry fee," said organizer Mahina Chillingworth, noting that WSL had stepped up to fund the women's teams. "There's no doubt these powerful wahine were the highlight of the whole Backdoor Shootout."

Outstanding performers included Kennelly, North Shore local goofy foot Moana Jones Wong, and Kaua'i native Bethany Hamilton. A mother of three, Hamilton is one of the most impressive, high-performance surfers in the world, despite having lost her left arm to a shark bite at age thirteen.

In February 2022, Moana Wong won the debut women's Billabong Pro Pipeline, with Moore placing second. Watching the women surf big, barreling Pipeline was "incredibly exciting and unforgettable,"

said Eric Logan, CEO of WSL, adding the event was also "the most-watched CT season-opener."

Costa Rica's Brisa Hennessy took first place in the debut women's Hurley Pro Sunset Beach, with Kaua'i world tour veteran Malia Manuel placing second. Manuel, Moore, and rookies Bettylou Sakura Johnson, Luana Silva, and Gabriela Bryan represented Hawai'i on the 2022 world tour; only Moore and an astonishing Bryan (ranked world #9) survived the mid-season cut.

On the South Shore in June, WSL inaugurated a qualifying series event in at Ala Moana Bowls, with ninety-six male and only twenty-four female contestants. During a good-size summer swell, Moana Wong took first place, and seventeen-year-old Puamakamae DeSoto of Mākaha came in second. A wave of other up-and-coming Hawai'i shortboarders includes Zoe McDougall, Frankie Harrer, Eweleiula Wong, Erin Brooks, Nora Liotta, and Keala Tomoda-Bannert.

The 2022 CT wrapped in great style, with a winner-take-all final heat at Lower Trestles, California, when number-one-ranked Carissa Moore was defeated by Stephanie Gilmore, who took her record, eighth world title.

Overlooked for years as old-fashioned by many, longboarding has been experiencing a rejuvenating revival, thanks in large part to young women's appreciation of an organic, cool, flowing style, going with the wave instead of slashing and hacking.

WSL Longboard Tour standouts in 2022 included Hawai'i's Kelis Kaleopaa, who placed second behind winner U.S. surfer Soleil Errico; Sophia Culhane, who placed third; and three-time world champ Honolua Blomfield (fourth); Sally Cohen (12th) and Kirra Seale (19th). Two-time world champ Kelia Moniz took time off while expecting her second child. Other Hawai'i contenders include Keani Canullo, Haley Otto, Luluhia Blomfield Kane, Tiki Willis, Kalina Jones, and Megan Godinez.

Also making surfing news, Maui longboarder Sierra Lerback became the first woman to win against a field of men in the prestigious Old Mal division in the 2022, Noosa Festival of Surfing in Australia.

Still, despite all this progress, a wide gap between genders remains. In 2023, there were thirty-four men and eighteen women admitted to the World Surf League championship tour.

Asked about the disparity, "The CT competitor numbers are reflective of our membership base and as those grow we'll continue to evaluate," Logan said. "I'm proud of the strides we've made to date, we know that there is still more work to be done."

"There's still so much more that needs to be done before true equity is reached, I hope I live to see it," Betty Depolito said.

That hope grew exponentially bigger and brighter in January 2023, when the world saw and celebrated women surfing in the storied Eddie Aikau Big-Wave Invitational at Waimea Bay.

TRAILBLAZERS

# CHAPTER 7

# OBSTACLES

Everyone acknowledges catching a wave is the hardest part of surfing. It requires timing, judgment, placement, and all-out paddling, not to mention jockeying for position with other surfers. For female surfers, getting a wave can be doubly fraught on a watery playing field where we're outnumbered four to one by males.

"It's because I'm a girl I've felt it my whole life," Debbie Millikan said. "I can tell by the look in their eyes that most men assume I don't know how to surf and won't catch the wave."

← One small day at Tongg's, a man commits the etiquette breach of snaking against a woman who is surfing the wave. A surfer who is already up and riding has priority, a snake claims false priority by taking off closer to the peak, but too late. Photo by Dennis Oda

They're assuming wrong. Debbie is one of the best surfers of any gender at Suis, our neighborhood break. She's also the best of neighbors, who drops off home-made meals during times of sickness and loss, and offers to grocery shop for those at elevated risk during a pandemic.

The director of sustainability at Punahou School, Debbie earned a PhD in marine biology from the University of California at San Diego. Married to a fellow scientist, with a college-age son and daughter, she helped start the school gardening and farm-to-cafeteria programs at Waikiki Elementary School.

She is one of the most energetic, positive, community-building people I know, but even Debbie can't prevent the occasional bad-energy bomb in the surf.

"This guy dropped in on me three times in a row when I was in the right spot, I was deeper," she said. "He'd catch a wave, paddle back out and do it again. So finally I said, 'Oh, how was my wave?' And then he started yelling, 'Any wave I paddle for is mine!'"

↑ During a big summer 2022 swell at Ala Moana Bowls, a man commits the most egregious breach of surf etiquette—dropping in on a wave on which a woman is already up and riding, well-positioned in the pocket. She also has priority as she is closest to the peak. Photo by Craig T. Kojima/Honolulu Star-Advertiser

I've seen Debbie call men out for their bullying behavior towards others, including youngsters. Once a middle-aged man yelled at her teenage daughter. Often when she speaks up the wrongdoers turn their wrath on her with verbal abuse. I've paddled over and sat next to her to show support, and she has done the same for me.

Initially, however, Debbie was reluctant to talk about male-female harassment for this book. I was surprised, but then I understood. It's painful to remember cruelty. The hurt and humiliation come back. It was hard for my sister-in-law, Anne Wallace, to revisit the abuse she had suffered, but she told her story as a warning to me. She was one of the first people I knew who taught me that stories can protect us.

One early morning in her early twenties, out surfing alone at Huntington Beach, California, where she had ridden waves since childhood with her family, Anne was set upon with no warning and beaten up by several male surfers, complete strangers. She was the only woman in the water, and she was a gifted, all-around athlete; she could easily have been the best surfer in the lineup that day, and I've often wondered if that was why the men attacked.

Men were always drawn to Anne, usually not violently. She was quiet, gentle, and unaware that she was beautiful: blond, with clear hazel eyes, long legs, broad shoulders, and a curvy but slender build. I hated having to wear thick, heavy wetsuits in the frigid California sea, but Anne liked her full suit because it hid her body from the male gaze. The most shocking thing about the attack, she told me, breaking into tears, was that they hit her in the breasts. The pain was nearly unbearable. Then they held her underwater, nearly drowning her. But she fought for her life and managed to get away, riding the whitewater in to the beach.

> I CAN TELL BY THE LOOK IN THEIR EYES THAT MOST MEN ASSUME I DON'T KNOW HOW TO SURF AND WON'T CATCH THE WAVE.
>
> – DEBBIE MILLIKAN

As Debbie and I talked it over, we realized that constant sexual discrimination in the water had worn us both down. Thinking about it made us feel upset, so we repressed the memories. And we didn't like to admit it, but sometimes we felt afraid when men harassed us, and fear has a chilling effect on speech.

"I guess I've just gotten so used to it that I sometimes don't want to think or talk about how we are constantly having to prove ourselves," Debbie said. "But in the end, I know I've always got to speak up for what's right."

# Carissa Moore has also spoken up about gender

imbalance and its inhibiting effects. "Surfing has been a very male-dominated sport," she told my colleague, Ferd Lewis, at the *Honolulu Star-Advertiser* in September, 2018. "When I first started out, I was the only girl in the lineup at times. Sometimes it is still a struggle to get waves with all the guys out there," added the then-three-time world champ.

Carissa Moore at Kewalos. Photos by Craig T. Kojima/Honolulu Star-Advertiser

Ferd's article reported World Surf League would start paying equal prize money to women and men in 2019. Carissa praised the move but also addressed the inequity females face in recreational surfing.

Later that month, when she returned to the islands after winning the first-ever championship tour event to be held in a wave pool, at California's Surf Ranch, I asked Carissa to elaborate on the struggle.

"It just can be intimidating at times," she said. "Males out in the lineup are stronger, more aggressive, and sometimes it's hard to stand up and take ownership, meet that intensity."

That's why she's always glad to get back to Kewalos, her home break. "It's pretty friendly. I've been surfing there my whole life, and get some respect there."

For newer, non-local surfers, like UH student Izzie Cleofe, respect is harder to find.

Once, when she protested after a guy cut her off, a whole group of males chimed in to belittle her surfing. "They said, 'Why you haven't caught one yet?' I said, 'Because he cut me off!' Then he said he couldn't have cut me off because it was his wave. I felt very judged," Izzie said.

I remembered the story a friend told me when I asked why she didn't surf, although she'd grown up by Kailua Beach. When she was a kid in the 1970s, she said, her sister was the only girl who surfed at Kailua shorebreak, "and she was better than the boys, which they hated." One day, "a boy deliberately shot the point of his board deep into her leg muscle and it got badly infected." Her sister quit surfing, and my friend never started.

Male entitlement is a problem not only with strangers, but with friends, added Mikayla Brennan. "With girlfriends, we want to make sure we all have a good time, but when you go surfing with guy friends, you're on your own. They want to catch everything. They'll even say it's your wave, and then they'll take it."

"At (Ala Moana) Bowls, the men are all acting like 'it's my turn,' all in a line," said Wendy Sakuma, age twenty. "Local boys think this is their territory and I understand that," added the California native, "but they should share. On the beach, guys can be so sweet, but when they get out in the water, there's a difference."

Izzie summed it up. "Guys in the water have a lot of pride, and their egos come out. They're more focused on catching the biggest, baddest wave, not on having fun.

Their friend, Mikayla Brennen, recounted an incident at the Waikīkī spot Number Threes, a fast, challenging, premium break. "I was paddling for a wave when I saw a surfer was already on it, so I didn't go, but he yelled at me anyway," Mikayla said. "He was really scary, super intimidating, paddling up to me and my friend, a guy who had also accidentally got in his way."

Mikayla apologized repeatedly, but the man kept shouting. "He said beginners shouldn't be on these waves, but later we noticed he was a surf instructor, he was teaching beginners right there at Threes!"

He didn't sound like a legitimate surf teacher to me. The beachboy concessions and other companies providing surf lessons at Waikīkī hold legally required com-

Bethany Hamilton surfing the North Shore of O'ahu.

Coco Ho Surfing in the Hawaiian Pro Surf Contest in Hale'iwa, Hawai'i at the 2010 Triple Crown of Surfing.

Anna Fry surfi Rocky Point o North Shore of C

mercial permits and licenses. But if you have a complaint, never confront a sketchy surf instructor directly, advised Meghan Statts, director of the state Division of Boating and Ocean Recreation in the Hawai'i Department of Land and Natural Resources. Call the Division of Conservation and Resources Enforcement at 643-DLNR (3567), and give a description of the teacher and the place and time, and DOCARE will investigate, she said.

Hawai'i women surfers I've spoken with share the hope that things are getting better and more equal for every new generation as they follow in the wake of trailblazing pioneers from Rell Sunn, Joey Hamasaki, Margo Oberg, and Rochelle Ballard to Bethany Hamilton, Carissa Moore, Coco Ho, Malia Manuel, Honolua Blomfield, and Kelia Moniz. But veteran North Shore surf event organizer "Banzai" Betty Depolito, who co-founded the first all-women Hawai'i big wave event at Waimea Bay, said a large gender gap remains at all levels of the sport, with males outnumbering females from children's menehune contests to the world championship tour. There will be no surf equity, Depolito said, until gender numbers and opportunities are equal.

Conversations with younger surfers confirm that equality is still far from reality.

On the North Shore in April 2017, I spoke with local surfer Mahina Maeda, then age nineteen, who had won the 2016 Wahine Pipe Pro, a qualifying series event. She said she had been practicing early that morning out at Rocky Point, "It was perfect Rockys until the boys came out," Mahina said with a smile and a shrug, but her dark eyes flashed with anger.

A few days later, the World Surf League held the 2017 Wahine Pro on a beautiful clear day in glassy, peeling, 4- to 6-foot Pipeline waves that the women charged, performing barrels, aerials—the works—with stunning grace.

"It's a little easier when there's not a bunch of boys in the lineup," the girl winner, Frankie Harrer, commented on WSL's website.

One might think the number of women had been growing in order to produce the 2022 record crop of three Hawai'i female rookies on the WSL championship tour. But no, said rookies Luana Silva and Bettylou Sakura Johnson, O'ahu North Shore natives and best friends, who were seventeen and sixteen years old, respectively, when they qualified for the tour along with Kaua'i native Gabriela Bryan, age nineteen.

Luana and Bettylou told me they were usually the only girls their age in the lineups during recreational, or free, surf sessions. "There were definitely not a lot of girls when I was a kid," a quietly exhilarated Bettylou told me after she won the 2021 Haleiwa Challenge contest, defeating her role model Carissa Moore. "It used to be just me and Lulu (Silva) on the North Shore, and then the CT (championship tour) girls."

Now, though, things have changed, Bettylou said. "These last couple years, there's a huge boom of younger girls."

While that's promising for women's surf equity on the North Shore, Hale'iwa, I haven't seen many younger girls surfing in town. Nor has eleven-year-old Cappy Makaiau who said she sees mostly boys and men and women in their twenties and older in the lineups she frequents at Kewalos and Ala Moana Beach Park.

↑ (left to right) Jenn Marr, Betty Depolito, Kelly Kennelly, and Carol Philips. Photo by Craig T. Kojima/Honolulu Star-Advertiser

↑ North Shore Surf Girls instructor, Betty Depolito, catches a wave during a surf lesson at Chun's Reef in Hale'iwa, O'ahu. Photo by Jamm Aquino/Honolulu Star-Advertiser

Asked whether anyone cuts her off in surf sessions, "My brother," Cappy said, referring to her younger brother, age ten. "Literally every wave I take, he'll try to catch it. And my father," she added, turning to Jarad Makaiau, who sat beside her on a picnic bench in Mākālei Beach Park as they hydrated after a surf session. "Dad will say 'go,' but then he'll be in the way."

"No! I never do that," Jarad said.

"Yes! You just did it again out there," Cappy said, pointing seaward.

"That's because I'm teaching you, you gotta learn to navigate around people," he said with a smile.

"But I couldn't go around you, there was no room," his daughter said. "You were right there!"

As Cappy and Jarad bantered, it was obvious how close and comfortable together they felt. I was reminded of Bunky Bakutis, who taught and surfs with his daughters Ane and Helena, Bill and Kiana Blankenfeld, and of George Downing sending his daughter Kai'ulu on the best wave of her life. The first teachers for Carissa Moore, Coco Ho, and many other top female surfers have included their dads.

HAWAI'I WOMEN SURFERS SHARE THE HOPE THAT THINGS ARE GETTING BETTER AND MORE EQUAL FOR EVERY NEW GENERATION AS THEY FOLLOW IN THE WAKE OF TRAILBLAZING PIONEERS.

Cappy Makaiau and her dad, Jarad, paddle in together.
Photo by Dennis Oda

"WOMEN COME AND GO IN THE LINEUP MORE THAN MEN BECAUSE ONCE WE HAVE KIDS, THE RESPONSIBILITIES OF CHILD CARE FALL ON US."

— CATHERINE TOTH FOX

Other girls paddle out and learn together by trial and error; some have lessons from family friends. But Catherine Toth Fox was self-taught and started late, in her twenties, by paddling out at Waikīkī all alone.

"I always wanted to surf," Cat told me, but she lacked the opportunity, growing up in Kalihi Valley above downtown Honolulu. At Roosevelt High School, where she played land sports such as soccer, volleyball, and tennis, her group of friends included boys who surfed, "and we girls would tag along, hang on the beach and watch."

Why didn't she borrow a board from one of the boys and try? "It didn't occur to me," Cat replied. "At the time, in the late 80s early 90s, it was mostly boys paddling out. Girls cruised on the beach, frolicked in the water."

Finally, after she had completed college and graduate school, got a job and a car, Toth "decided I was really going to commit, do it regularly, and master the sport."

She got a surfboard, learned something about ocean conditions from talking with the Waikīkī beachboys, and started paddling out at Queens and Canoes before dawn at least three days a week. "I was like the only girl paddling out at that time of day, and the youngest person in the lineup by forty years," she said. "It was all old guys on longboards."

And today, more than twenty years since she started out, "I'm still one of the only females in the early, early morning," she said. "I think men treat women very differently in the water. And I don't like it."

Both men and women feel territorial in the surf, she said, but men have more leverage because they're able to simply be there more, "the rooted veterans in the spot." That's because they have fewer demands on their time. "Women come and go in the lineup more than men because once we have kids, the responsibilities of child care fall on us," said Cat, who is married and has a young son, Landon. "Priorities shift and we're not seen as much."

As rooted regulars in the lineup, men exert control by doling out waves, according to their whims, to women of their choice. It's the old paradigm of divide and con-

Debbie and daughter, Kalae Millikan, Sydney Iaukea, and Mindy Pennybaker chat at Mākālei Beach Park before hitting the waves. Photo by Cindy Ellen Russell/Honolulu Star-Advertiser

quer. It leads, Cat and Sydney Iaukea said, to entitlement among females who assume their youthful, pretty faces and figures will induce males to give them waves.

"I mean I don't mind it, young girls trying to get favors, but when we were girls, we never thought about being cute in the surf," Sydney said. "Of course, there were no cameras, no Instagram."

Cat prefers to choose her own waves rather than be given them, often at the last moment, in which case it's not a real gift, but a leftover. Often, a man might assert priority for a wave if he's sitting deepest, that is closest to the peak, but, after paddling, sees he's going to miss it or it's going to close out on him. So he yells at someone else, sometimes a woman who was in the right position, to "go." But this is all happening in a split second, and your timing is already thrown off if you try, usually too late, for a leftover.

"When a guy tells me go, go, paddle harder, it's very patronizing," Cat said. "But what also annoys me is, so many good female surfers let male surfers give them breaks."

This leads to a breakdown of traditional order and courtesy in the lineup, with women feeling entitled to breach surf etiquette and drop in on anyone "because they've been invited to" by others, in the past.

"I had to earn my spot in the lineup," Cat said, by waiting her turn and surfing well. "I'm certainly not going to sit there in the impact zone in my bikini, looking helpless."

At Waikīkī, she often sees girls who paddle out, bringing photographers with them, trying to be lifestyle influencers with a surfing theme, for which "you don't have

↑ Late afternoon surfers at Queen's in Waikīkī. Photo by Mindy Pennybacker

to be good, you just have to be cute." She sees other girls who paddle out with their surf video cameras but don't catch any waves.

Men aren't expected to look sexy while they surf. Instead of buttock-baring thongs, they wear long, baggy shorts. But women have long felt pressured to maintain toned, perfect bodies to show off in revealing swim- and surfwear.

In interviews and in her 2018 short film *Riss,* Carissa Moore acknowledged the toll of societal pressures and expectations, and how she at times has been intensely self-critical and suffered from low self-esteem. With humor, compassion, and honesty, she recounts how she has freed herself from the negative feedback loop and the male gaze, while focusing on keeping her life in balance between work, family, and play. The mission of her Moore Aloha foundation is to help girls and women feel love and pride for who they are, just as they are, and develop the skills and confidence to pursue their dreams. One of Carissa's sponsors is the clothing brand Hurley, with whom she collaborates to design and test her own line of high-performance surf suits that are stylish and sexy without letting it all hang out.

"Surfing has been sold as a commodity and a lifestyle brand," Cat said, adding those who buy into it "are missing out on the best part of surfing. I want to tell them, put your camera down, feel the rhythm of the ocean and the wind."

There are many obstacles to women's surfing, but we are overcoming them through solidarity and sisterhood, telling our own stories in our own voices, taking turns surfing and watching each other's children, and speaking up for what's right.

## Championship tour standout Johanne Defay

of France and big-wave champion Keala Kennelly of Hawai'i have spoken about being rejected by sponsors because of their looks. They have had to scrimp and sacrifice to pay their own way to competitions.

In July 2021, Defay, then en route to represent France in the debut Olympic surfing event, reminisced about being dropped by Roxy, the women's clothing company, leaving her sponsorless early in her career. "They were just like 'Oh, you don't look this way, you know, for, like, pictures," Defay said in an interview with the Associated Press, "and I just felt like I was never doing enough or I wasn't fitting in, in the way that they wanted for their brand."

In the same article, Carissa Moore was quoted about having felt insecure about her looks. "Everyone had this idea of what a surfer girl should look like. And there were a lot of 'hot lists' or the 'cutest surfer girl list. I never made them," she said. She has also spoken about alternately starving herself and binge eating as a teenager.

# CHAPTER 8

# ADVICE

It's game-changing when girls and women strategize about systemic discrimination in surfing and how to get around it. Simply by talking with other female surfers, I've gained confidence and perspective that have helped me better negotiate in the waves. Sharing stories has been a great reality check: Other females have confirmed that yes, I'm not imagining even the most unbelievably rude behaviors; yes, gender bias does surround us every day. I feel more relaxed, patient and liberated in the lineup now I know I'm not alone. I'm emerging from a cocoon I thought was protecting me, but was actually a trap that cut me off and hemmed me in.

← After surfing Suis (Suicides) for the first time, (front to back) Wendy Sakuma, Isabel "Izzie" Cleofe, May Kamaka, and Mikayla Brennan exit the water near Mākālei Beach Park. Photo by Dennis Oda

The other day out at Suis, amid a crowd of twenty-five in a building summer swell, conditions were windy, shifty, and chaotic. But on a bright note, there were more women than usual—six of us. True, the ratio was still four to one, but there were enough to make up a spontaneous posse, including regulars Andree Paradis, Cristal Mortensen, Lecia "Dodie" Lau, and a couple of other girls whose faces were familiar but whose names I didn't know. I'm going to be sure and introduce myself in calmer circumstances.

As the guys battled each other frantically for waves, taking off too deep into closeouts or missing waves despite a frantic effort, while paddling around us as a matter of course, we girls sat in a wide circle, observing the chaos and exchanging ironic glances, "oh-well" shrugs, and philosophical smiles. We didn't join in the male battle: One could easily get hurt, with beginners, aggressive, gawky youngsters, and old, wobbly neighborhood guys all going out of control. We ladies waited patiently, noting when certain men missed waves we could have taken, and encouraging one another to be ready to seize our chance when they missed the next one. I sat apart from the crowd, off to one side, and eventually a wave came straight to me and I hopped on it. I only got three waves to myself, but they were nice, long, splashy rides, and on the third I went all the way in, reminding myself not to be greedy or push my luck in crowded, sketchy conditions.

These days, I feel fortified by the wisdom of other surfing, working moms, who say they no longer care so much how many waves they ride, but feel happy and refreshed just to get out in the ocean.

I'm learning attitude makes all the difference. With every wave females ride, we're not only having fun but scoring cumulative reparations for sexism. It's time to lose any grudges and hankerings for revenge, which blow things out of proportion and only drag you down. Besides, anger raises stress levels, which is bad for the health.

My new motto: Surfing well—with a smile—is the best redress.

Here are some tips for recreational surfers of all levels that can help you surf better and have more fun.

First and above all, be prepared and safe. That might seem incompatible with surfing as an inherently risk-taking activity, but it's not. It's all relative, of course. After some near-death experiences, most big-wave surfers now wear flotation vests,

Jenny Van Gieson surfs Ala Moana Bowls. Photo by Paul Teruya

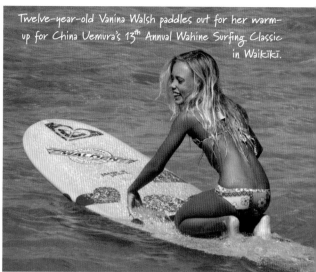

Twelve-year-old Vanina Walsh paddles out for her warm-up for China Uemura's 13th Annual Wahine Surfing Classic in Waikīkī.

↑ The ultimate chill contestant in the 45th Annual Buffalo Big Board Surfing Classic in Mākaha, O'ahu.

Paddling out to surfing hotspot at Hoʻokipa Beach, Maui.

an innovation that was designed and tested by their colleagues. At the first Pipeline women's championship tour event, held in 2022 in overhead waves barreling over the shallow reef, most of the contestants wore helmets.

Make sure you're a strong swimmer in rough, open-ocean conditions, not just a pool, as leashes—and boards—can break, advises Kailua resident Kiana Blankenfeld, a surf instructor and former surf shop manager.

Next, fortify yourself with knowledge before paddling out: If you're a beginner, have some—not just one—lessons under your belt. And no matter what your level of skill, never paddle out oblivious to daily conditions and underlying structure at a surf break: wave size and forecast; the tide; how shallow the bottom is; location of rocks, jetties, reefs and exposed coral heads, current and wind directions and speed.

Choosing when to go out is crucial. "Check the surf report, and never go out on the ocean without checking the weather. We can't control nature," Kiana said.

Be sure to familiarize yourself with a surf break where you've never gone before, or haven't been out for a long time. "Do your research before you go out," said Blankenfeld, who's also a mother of two and a UFC coach and gym manager. "Don't go out without any knowledge of that spot, and if it's a new spot, it's always better to go with people familiar with that area."

It's a good habit to sit on shore and watch for at least twenty minutes, until a set comes through, says Mark Cunningham, a champion bodysurfer and retired Honolulu City and County lifeguard who was stationed for decades at Pipeline. Follow the Hawai'i lifeguards' motto, "When in doubt, don't go out." You are not going to have fun if you are in terror of your life, paralyzed by fear, and if others have to risk their lives coming to your rescue.

"You gotta go when you're ready," Kiana said. "When in doubt don't go out, that's so true: If you're unsure, you could get hurt, or feel stuck—I've had those experiences going out on my own."

Meghan Van Ness walks the nose, with a hang five in her sights, on O'ahu's North Shore. Photo by Mei-Li Restani, Surfing Moms

Anna Shoemaker gives her child a kiss during a Surfing Moms outing at Kailua Beach. Photo by KC Lostetter Photography, Surfing Moms

That goes for taking others out, too. Taking a child surfing when they're not ready can result in a lifelong fear of the ocean and waves. Wait until they say they want to try.

"My two girls are six and nine," Kiana said. "My older one, I've taken her surfing, and she loves it, has gone out a few times on her own, on her little wavestorm board. I'm waiting for my six-year-old to tell me when she's ready."

If you're a beginner, take a lesson—more than one. After being initially surprised by new people showing up at Surfing Moms sessions with no experience of surfing and the expectation that they would learn on the spot, the nonprofit now asks would-be members to take surf lessons first, founder Elizabeth Madin said.

"We started getting people who were wanting to learn, but there was a high potential for incidents, and enough going on already, between surfing and the moms keeping an eye on the kids on the beach," Elizabeth said.

↑ Surfing Moms Alyssa Myers, Kristi Hallock, Elizabeth Madin, KC Lostetter, and the group's children socialize on Kailua Beach. Photo by KC Lostetter Photography, Surfing Moms

"We now make it clear on our website that we actually cannot teach you to surf, we're not instructors, and recommend if people want to come, at least take a few lessons first."

She added lessons can be fun and at a minimum, help neophytes feel more comfortable and confident in the water. "For her thirteenth birthday party, my daughter wanted to have her friends come with her for a surf lesson," Elizabeth said. "We did it with Kiana Blankenfeld, at Castles, in front of Kaimana Beach Park, which was really nice—we recommend Kiana as an instructor to people interested in joining Surfing Moms."

"My surf lesson is very different than your typical tourist, 'I want to catch a wave' lesson," Kiana said, adding she doesn't share the goal many teachers guarantee, that students will stand up on their first ride.

"First, we sit on the sand, and I explain what we're looking at. Observe how many people are in the water; where the rocks are; where the current's pulling from; where people are paddling out and back in." Visually locating the lineup, "we look at who's catching the most waves and where are they taking off from? Usually they always go to the same spot."

With regard to staying in the takeoff zone, "we look at how quickly people are drifting down the beach and how hard they have to paddle back up-current," Kiana said. "Surfing is ninety percent paddling, and ten percent catching waves."

Because falling is intrinsic to beginning surfing—you're tumbling more than you're riding at first—"We go over how to fall properly," she said. "If you're gonna fall, always fall with the idea that it's shallow underneath you. That way, you won't hit the reef."

During a group surf session at Waialua on O'au's North Shore, Surfing Moms members Lindsay Hedman, Kirsten Olsen, Meghan Van Ness, Elizabeth Madin, Amelia Borofsky, Amanda Shaw, and Rochelle Ziegler join hands in solidarity. Photo by Mei-Li Restani. Surfing Moms

Fall flat and limp, "like a starfish," she tells her students. "Stay on top of the water. Don't dive."

Still on land, lying on a board, they practice paddling motions and "the typical pop up," pushing up in one smooth movement to their feet. Once in the water, before paddling out, they practice rolling the board under, holding tight to the rails, to use it as a shield against the impact of a breaking wave or oncoming surfer.

Then, as they paddle out, "I'm pointing out where we're going, how far out, and we pick landmarks out to sea and on the beach that you're going to line up with, that tell you when you're drifting in or out, or to the side."

You can learn by watching good surfers. "I tell them if they see a person who's catching the most waves, sit by their side and observe for a bit."

She also teaches her students to make eye contact, ask questions and communicate, not to assume that other surfers are aware they're trying for a wave. "I tell them to be vocal, make sure people in water know you're there."

Communicating, Kiana said, is crucial to getting along. "Basic surf etiquette, usually that's just asking questions. You're sitting on the shoulder (not the peak of the wave), saying I'm new here, asking questions, letting people know you want to learn, with the attitude of 'oh, I'm kinda new here, just feeling it out.' If people see that you're being humble and patient, then, in the culture of surfing, most people are, oh, let me help you out!"

In the process, you're also investing in a happier future by building relationships with the people who surf at that spot.

Frequently, when she lets regulars in the lineup know she's teaching a surf lesson, "people cheer (her students) on."

So long as they behave, that is. The other etiquette basics include waiting your turn instead of paddling for every wave, and taking care not to block or drop in on another surfer.

> "SURFING IS NINETY PERCENT PADDLING, AND TEN PERCENT CATCHING WAVES."
>
> — KIANA BLANKENFELD

"Don't go right in front of a person and turn around and catch a wave in front of them," Kiana said, drawing an analogy to road etiquette: "Don't speed up into traffic and cut somebody off right away. That's going to piss off a whole bunch of people."

Equally aggravating to local surfers is when tourists rent a board and go out without a lesson, without doing any research. "That's the lacking humility part," she said. "You hear a lot of old stories about top Hawaiian surfers like Eddie Aikau, Duke Kahanamoku, one thing they all have in common is, they've had interactions with people who are not from Hawai'i that are not humble, and in the end those people end up being humbled—either by the ocean or by the people who are part of that community."

I've learned through experience that locals like myself can save a lot of grief by being humble, too, especially when we venture out to unfamiliar breaks. I may be local off Diamond Head, but that doesn't lend me any cred at Mākaha or Hale'iwa. Attitude and behavior are the measure of an arriviste.

"How can we all get to a point when we can surf together and not have words?" asked Kim Heyer, who learned in the 1960s and has surfed her whole life at Tongg's. Kim misses the respectful climate of the old days "when kūpuna taught you take your turn, there's a right of way." She was taught by veteran surfers like her father, and world champion Fred Hemmings, that "you caught a wave, you come back out, you let someone else have one. If you're on the inside of the peak, you have the right of way going in that direction."

But new surfers don't seem to know etiquette anymore, Kim said, especially the new crop of hydrofoil surfers who now frequent Tongg's and pose an extra threat with the sharp, underwater blades of their hoverboards.

It can be infuriating when you're getting cut off by paddle arounds and dangerous when others drop in or paddle in front of you, but try to stay calm, Kiana Blankenfeld advises. "I've had people drop in on me and pretty and much knock me right off my feet, but you can't control people."

Her own teacher, her father and famed surfer Bill Blankenfeld, one of the original members of the Da Hui local surf club on O'ahu's North Shore, counsels staying cool. "When I look to my dad, he says 'Babe, they don't know what they're doing, you've got to have that laid back surfer attitude,'" Kiana said, "but if it was him I think he might have done something different."

"My parents always taught me to be polite, be patient, and I teach my daughters that, but as parents, we don't always practice what we preach."

# One of the best etiquette summaries

I've found is at Kale Brock's online surf school Thesurfersroadmap.com, one of many helpful resources featured from time to time on Hawaii's Surf News Network, surfnewsnetwork.com, which provides daily surf reports, news and videos.

Here's a checklist condensed from Brock's etiquette article.

Most important rule: Don't drop in. That's when a person who isn't closest to the peak, and doesn't have priority, takes a wave in front of someone else.

Take turns. The surfer who has been waiting longest in lineup has priority, or first choice, of waves that come in, Brock says.

Don't impinge on the priority holder's space. "Do not go and sit in the pocket when people are waiting (there)," Brock advises. "Sit a little bit wider and wait for that person (to have their turn)."

If the priority surfer doesn't take their turn, the next person in line has priority. If a person paddles for a wave and misses it, they've technically lost priority and should move to the back of the line. "But you can be kind" and let them try again, Brock reminds us.

Like Kiana, he says communication is essential. "If you're interested in a wave and someone's going for it, let them know (you're going)," he writes, but "if they keep going, let it go. Maybe they thought it was their turn." Maybe they didn't see you.

At the same time, Brock, like Debbie Millikan and other surfers I've spoken with, notes that most surfers are very conscious of the lineup and know their relative position.

If confronted with a repeat offender, Brock suggests you speak up: "Hey, I notice you just caught two waves in a row, would you mind sharing?" To this, however, I would add that you make sure you're not alone and have a safe distance.

Another "huge breach" is snaking, or paddling around. When a surfer has been waiting closest to the peak in priority position, "a huge breach is to paddle to the inside of this surfer's position and try to catch the wave that surfer wants." Instead of waiting their turn, the snake has cut the line by placing themselves "in the technical position of right of way, closest to the pocket, or the inside (of the peak)," Brock writes.

When paddling out, if a surfer is riding towards you, paddle towards the whitewater, not towards the shoulder in the direction the surfer is going. "You are crossing their path and may prevent them getting in the pocket, which is every surfer's goal." You might also get hit.

Hold onto your board. If you don't have enough space or time to avoid an oncoming surfer, roll under your board; don't ditch it.

Whether paddling out, recovering from a fall, or waiting in the linoup, do not take a sideways position in relation to the wave. "It increases the space you are taking up and chance of collision." It also makes it easier for a wave to wash you in out of control.

Her father taught her a drop-in is "acceptable if it's truly an accident and they say sorry, didn't see you," but they shouldn't keep doing it.

Founded in the 1970s by a group of Hawaiian surfers concerned about the growing exclusion of locals from prime surf breaks by contest organizers, Da Hui has worked to reclaim surfing as a Hawaiian cultural practice and instill respect and create opportunity for native surfers, particularly youth. Some of the members, known as the Black Shorts, were hired as in-water security by some contest promoters; club members developed their own Da Hui surf clothing brand and established an annual Da Hui Shootout contest at Pipeline that, in 2022, included women contestants for the first time. Previously, women had lacked sponsors to pay the entry fee, said event organizer Mahina Chillingworth.

↑ Kiana Blankenfeld at a secret surf spot on the East Side of O'ahu. Photo courtesy Kiana Blankenfeld

Her father was "my big role model growing up," Kiana said. "From the beach, I used to watch him surf huge waves. He has this very classic style. He's a really big, tall, dark Hawaiian guy, and from some people's perspective he can look intimidating, but his surfing is graceful, almost like Fred Flintstone doing twinkle toes when bowling."

As a father and mentor, Bill Blankenfeld helped his daughter transcend gender barriers by teaching her "how to understand the ocean, the safety (rules), and how to surf bigger waves that some people might consider more extreme, double your size."

Beyond these skills, Kiana reflected, perhaps his most meaningful teaching is to park your ego onshore: you really don't have to prove anything. "When I go surfing, I just go to have fun," she said. "My dad has always said just do it for you, we're not doing it to impress other people."

Once, she remembers, "This guy said, 'oh, you're really good,' and I asked my dad what he thought. He asked, 'What does good mean to you? Are you competing with yourself, or with other people?'"

Having decided she's surfing for herself, Kiana shrugs off compliments the way she tries to ignore drop-ins. "If guys are giving me compliments for whatever reason, I really don't care what they think."

And, she adds, that freedom and self-direction is what she wants for her daughters. "I tell them, don't let other people's judgments or thoughts affect the way you're going to run your life. I think that's a lesson young kids should all learn," especially because now, given social media's preoccupation with "likes" and curated self-image, "it's all about hitting the ground, impressing other people."

Because surf spots vary radically, it's also important to know where to go with your skill set. Waikīkī is overrun by beginners, which can be frustrating for everybody because the waves at some Waikīkī spots including Castles, Publics, Queens Surf, Populars, and Threes, are intermediate- to-advanced level and dangerous when it's big. The best breaks for beginners around Oʻahu are near-

Bethany Hamilton surfs Pipeline on Oʻahu's North
Shore in the 2022 Da Hui Backdoor Shootout.
Photo by Sean Davey

shore, inside breaks at Tongg's near Diamond Head; Canoes, Publics (where you'll see the surf school on the reef fronting Waikīkī Aquarium), Queens (just out from the sea wall, it's known as Baby Queens), and Pops. Good intermediate spots include Courts and Concessions off Ala Moana Regional Park; White Plains in 'Ewa Beach; Pōka'ī Bay in Wai'anae; Pua'ena Point and Chun's Reef in Hale'iwa (not Laniākea, with its freight-train currents), Inside Velzyland and Turtle Bay in Kahuku, on the North Shore; Lā'ie Bay on the Windward Shore; and Kailua Beach Park. Caveat: Beginners should steer clear of any break during high-surf advisories.

Beginners should also, at all times, avoid Kaisers and Rockpiles in front of the Waikīkī boat harbor, along with the radically fast-breaking Ala Moana Bowls with its famously truculent crowd. Resist any temptation to paddle to far-out reef breaks off unguarded beaches, such as Niu Valley and 'Āina Haina on the South Shore; Mokulē'ia, Kahuku, Lā'ie, Hau'ula and Ka'a'awa on the North and Windward Shores. At guarded beaches that receive big, powerful waves, notably Mākaha on the West Side and anywhere along the North Shore's "miracle mile," from Waimea Bay to Sunset Beach, don't paddle out when waves are higher than two feet Hawaiian (four feet faces) or, worst of all, on a rising swell.

Despite the offerings of surf adventure tours, big waves at Mākaha, Waimea Bay, or Sunset Beach and the shallow tubular breaks over toothy reefs at Off the Walls, Backdoors, Pipeline, Pūpūkea, and Rocky Point are definitely not, ever, for beginner or intermediate surfers. They're lethal and seriously for experts only.

For more information regarding surf breaks throughout the Hawaiian Islands, see John Clark's series of books including *Beaches of Hawaii*, and volumes focused on the beaches of O'ahu, Kaua'i/Ni'ihau, and Maui/Moloka'i. And ask the lifeguards at the tower about conditions on any given day.

Before taking a lesson, ask about a surf instructor's experience, references, whether they have CPR/lifesaving training, and whether they will stay close by and choose conditions suited to your skill level, advises Melissa Kurpinski, a Michigan native, who started surfing after moving to Hawai'i at age thirty-nine.

"I always wanted to surf," said Melissa, a hairstylist who lives and runs her salon in Kaimukī. "It was my childhood dream. In the 80s I was a latchkey kid watching old reruns of *Gidget* on TV."

She started visiting Hawai'i twice a year in her twenties, but couldn't see herself starting to surf here. "It was too intimidating. I was afraid. There was too much going on offshore," she correctly observed.

Finally she decided to take a lesson and ended up at a surf camp on the North Shore of O'ahu in February, the peak of big-wave season. "In five days, I only stood up on my board twice," she said. "The waves were just too big. There were maybe five other women, and they weren't learning either. We compared notes, we were all terrified." Not a surprise. The students hadn't known any better, of course, but the instructors should have.

"I realize now, looking back, that it probably wasn't an above-board surf school," Melissa said. After that,

↑ Surfer Melissa Kurpinkski at Suis.
Photo by Dennis Oda

Kim Yuson, left, and Mahina Maeda crank some power turns on a long beauty of a wave at Rocky Point on O'ahu's North Shore. "It was a crowded evening and they shared that wave," says photographer Christa Funk. Photo by Christa Funk

she headed with a long board to the classic beginner break of Canoes, at Waikīkī, which is now her regular spot.

There are many long-established, reputable surf schools and teachers all around O'ahu's shores. They include the Hans Hedemann Surf School at Turtle Bay and other resorts; Ohana Surf Project in front of Waikīkī Aquarium; Aloha Beach Services in front of the Moana Surfrider Resort, run by Didi Robello, son of founder Harry Robello, one of the original Waikīkī Beach Boys and great-grand-nephew of Duke Kahanamoku; Waikiki Beach Services in front of the Royal Hawaiian Resort; and Moniz Family Surf on Ulunui Avenue in Waikīkī near Kūhiō Beach—famed waterman Tony Moniz and his wife, Tammy, teach surfing with their older sons, Micah and Isaiah. Their daughter, Kelia, a two-time world longboarding champion, and their sons, Seth (a championship tour shortboarder) and Josh (a contender on the shortboard qualifying and challenger series), compete on the world circuit. On Kaua'i, there's the Margo Oberg Surf School in Po'ipū, founded and still headed by the six-time world champ.

Melissa Kurpinski said she's happy surfing at Canoes because of the inclusive, lighthearted atmosphere. She's made friends in the lineup she sees regularly, which makes her feel she belongs to a community.

As Elizabeth Madin said, surfing is a real time network.

When you're among friends, or have a friendly attitude, it's easier to share and have fun. Kiana Blankenfeld said, "Catch as many waves as you can, and enjoy it, but remember, you don't need to be the person catching all the waves."

For Hawai'i women, surfing is about relationships and knowing our place, not in the sense of being kept down, but by understanding and respecting, in all its elemental and living complexity, the slice of ocean from where we take off and to which we return.

# Choose a surfboard that fits

The fun—and maddening—part of selecting a surfboard is the endless possibilities in nose (pointed or round), length, width, thickness, rocker (scoop), rails (the sides of the board), bottom configuration (flat or V-shaped), and tail. These choices should be dictated by a surfer's knowledge, skill, and the size of waves and kind of breaks where they plan to ride the board, according to Keone Downing of Downing Hawaii, Hawai'i's oldest surf shop, founded in 1949 by his father George Downing, the late big-wave pioneer.

"You want a surfboard that lets you have fun, be safe, and progress (improve)," said Keone, a graduate of the California College of the Arts, who shapes all Downing Hawaii's boards by hand.

When designing boards for women, "there's an adaptation that needs to take place, knowing a girl isn't as strong in the upper body as a guy for the most part," he said. "Women are stronger in the lower body and legs, but also lighter and tend to be smaller in stature."

While the average person needs a wider board than competitive surfers, because "wider boards are more stable and float better," Keone and his father discovered that for women's boards, the key is a narrower tail.

"Girls were coming into the shop asking for longboards with more rocker, because as they took off on a wave they were pearling (the nose plunging underwater)," Keone said. "But after analyzing it, Dad and I saw the problem wasn't the rocker, it was that when the women were taking off and got to their feet, they were too light to sink the tail and make the nose come up."

The Downings designed a mini longboard, between 7'3" to 7'11" long, with a round nose, but a narrow tail, so a woman could make late drops and take control of the tail when she stood up, and surf it in the pocket like a shortboard," Keone said.

The "minihune" longboards are one of Downing Hawaii's best sellers.

# Evolution of surfboards and women's surfing

Skegless, hardwood longboards 10 to 14 feet long, hewn from the trunks of tall trees and weighing up to 175 lbs., were used in pre-western Hawai'i, but there were also lighter models, such as Princess Ka'iulani's slender 7'4" board in the collection of the Bishop Museum.

Wooden boards remained standard until the 1940s but were generally too heavy and cumbersome for most women, according to California native Joe Quigg, known as the father of the modern surfboard.

Women's surfing took off after World War II with the invention of petrochemical plastics and foam, materials used to make much lighter, more maneuverable longboards, Quigg said during a panel discussion at the 2018 Honolulu Surf Film Festival.

Addressing his fellow panelists and Hawai'i surfing greats, "I hate to put down you men, but you guys really were running the women off of the waves," Quigg said.

"In 1946, I came out with the idea of a plastic surfboard, (using) fiberglass and plastic foam, (and) the beauty was it was super light, so I made boards for the girls and it caught on."

Not only that, but "the girls got so good on these foam boards that they were going circles around the men on their old, heavy longboards, and in fact

it caused a new style of riding," Quigg said to cheers from women in the audience.

In 1958, Hobie Alter and Gordon Clark invented polyurethane foam boards coated with fiberglass. As a result, "there was a huge increase in women's surfing in the early 60s," said Steve Morgan, who shapes for Hawaii Island Creations and Brewer Morgan Surfboards. "Guys surf more from their legs, while girls surf more from their hips," and the lighter synthetic boards with single fins, "were easier to pivot from the hips."

In 1967, "mini-guns," the same shape but shorter than the long, narrow, pointed "guns" big-wave surfers ride, by Hawai'i shaper Dick Brewer ushered in a shortboard revolution.

In the 1970s, Lynne Boyer, Jericho Poppler, Rell Sunn, Margo Oberg, and many other women, excelled on the era's pointed nose, mid length (7' or longer), narrow, single-fin boards with long, downturned rails that facilitated surfing with fluidity.

But, in the 1980s and early 1990s, surfers shredded and ripped the waves on extremely thin and narrow, three-fin thrusters sometimes called "potato chip" boards.

Into the aughts, "as surfboard design started to shorten and widen, it started to become a lot more dynamic for women," veteran pro surfer Rochelle Ballard told the surfing website Magic Seaweed in 2022.

After having long been eclipsed by shortboards, longboards had a renaissance among young women, thanks to new, thinner and lighter designs that made it easier to perform maneuvers, Steve Morgan said.

In the current shortboard arena, expert surfers are using shorter, narrower boards with straighter sides, which allow more speed, quicker rail-to-rail surfing, and getting through critical sections, Keone Downing said.

"Women can ride pretty small, light boards," Matt Biolos of Mayhem Surfboards said in a 2015 interview for *Surfer* magazine. "They're usually not as strong as men, so they need a little board with more rocker and a narrower tail block that they can whip around and turn" to catch a wave.

But if you're a recreational surfer, don't get ahead of yourself. "The average person needs a wider board than competitors," Downing said.

## Some Hawaiʻi surfboard & surfwear co.s

- arakawasurfboards.com
- downingsurf.com
- hawaiiansouthshore.com
- hawaiisurffactory.com
- inter-island.com
- kazumasurfboards.com
- localmotionhawaii.com
- surfboardfactoryhawaii.com/hic-brand
- patagonia.com/stores/hi/Haleiwa
- patagonia.com/stores/hi/Honolulu
- pyzelsurfboards.com
- surfnsea.com
- tcsurf.com

**Note:** Some surf shops also sell swim fins and bodyboards, rent surfboards, and offer lessons.

CHAPTER 9

# MĀLAMA HAWAIʻI

In addition to enjoying the waves, Hawaiʻi waterwomen are also active in their communities. They're advocating for gender equity, preserving public beach access and cultural sites, learning and respecting Hawaiian traditions, and protecting the natural environment, including the coral reefs that shape our waves.

Hawaiian values teach how to live in balance with nature, said cultural adviser Uʻilani Macahio, and the practice of heʻe nalu is about more than fun—call it serious fun. "It's not just to surf, it's to be an ocean woman, to understand the importance of taking care of the land as well as the ocean, because everything from land goes into the ocean."

With three other Big Island women, their husbands and partners, U'ilani co-founded a nonprofit community organization, Mālama I Ke Kai 'O Waipi'o (MaKa), after Hawai'i County suddenly closed the only road into the cliff-ringed, historic valley on the rugged, remote Hāmākua Coast in February 2022. The group filed a lawsuit on Earth Day, April 22, 2022, seeking the immediate reopening of this public road. It was closed by emergency order from Big Island Mayor Mitchell Roth citing the risk of fatal injury from falling rocks to users of the steeply inclined road. Valley residents, landowners, and farmers were allowed to continue to use the road, while nonresident users of the valley's public shoreline were barred.

In Hawai'i, however, the public has the right to access the shoreline, even, in some cases, across private property and in contravention of private landowners' development plans, under the state Constitution and case law based on traditional Hawaiian law and customary rights.

Waipi'o, with its river mouth sandbars and shorebreak along a black-pebble beach, was the nearest and most accessible surf spot for U'ilani and other residents of the rough Hāmākua Coast. Now they had been barred from the place where they not only surfed and bodysurfed, but fished and gathered, volunteered to help in the valley's extensive kalo fields, brought student groups to study Hawaiian culture, and, most of all, played. Play, including surfing, is essential to Hawaiian culture because it builds strength, provides relaxation, and stimulates out-of-the-box creative thinking, U'ilani said.

Being severed from Waipi'o beach was "really scary and really heartbreaking," said Heather Nakalu Kalei, a member of MaKa along with U'ilani,

↑ Waipi'o Valley Road leads down to the valley floor and Waipi'o Beach, composed of black pebbles and sand.

163

↑ U'ilani Macabio paddling out at Waipi'o Beach. Photo by Kia'i Tallett

↓ Sally Lundburg surfing at Waipi'o Beach. Photo by Sachi Cunningham

Sally Lundburg, Ariel Tergeoglou, Roland Shackelford, Patrick O'Leary, Jerry Bess, Travis Clark, Keith Tallett, and others. "I live in Waimea. My husband grew up surfing in Waipi'o. We were down there every week with our sons, ages one and three. Our sons should grow up there."

"It's our closest ocean access point," said filmmaker and high school art teacher Sally Lundburg, who cultivates a small organic kalo farm with her husband and teenage daughter. "We live in Pa'auilo Mauka. "I've been going to Waipi'o since I was a kid, starting surfing there in my twenties. We'd go at least several times a week, for sure. We are so busy, that's the time we connect with our community. Families barbecuing and watching kids play, talking story, getting exercise—no WiFi down there. Healthy food and farming are important, but there's also a nourishment that comes from playing together in nature, in the ocean, that feeds us in what we do during rest of week. We deeply feel the loss of each other, our community."

Prior to the closure, there had been no warning of imminent danger, nor any recent landslide or other change in the condition of Waipi'o Valley Road, Sally said. Nor had the public received notice or opportunity to comment. The lawsuit, filed by MaKa and fourteen individual Big Island residents, alleged Roth's decision was based on a flawed engineering report and "there appear to be no records of incidents of injury or death to persons from rock fall, landslide, or roadway failure along Waipi'o Valley Road at any time during the last fifty years."

On August 26, following a court-ordered mediation with MaKa, Mayor Roth amended his emergency order to open the road to Big Island residents, county-permitted tour company operators, and people seeking to practice their Native Hawaiian traditions, with access limited to vehicles with four-wheel drive—no pedestrians, equestrians, or bicycles/ATVs. In September incidents, taro farmers, kūpuna, lineal descendants of Waipi'o Valley, and community groups Protect Waipi'o Valley and Waipi'o Valley 'Ohana, blocked the road seeking to educate would-be visitors about overtourism's toll on the valley's ecosystem and cultural resources and encouraged them to turn back.

"It is clear that tourism is unacceptable to the Waipi'o Valley kūpuna, farmers, and 'ohana, and without a collaborative management plan in place, we support this refusal," MaKa president Roland Shackelford said in a press release.

On October 1, 2022, hundreds of Big Island residents gathered at the top of the valley road in a rally for ocean access organized by MaKa; as of press time, efforts were ongoing to create a mālama Waipi'o plan.

"There's so much we could do to mālama Waipi'o," Sally said. "An ocean person should always connect to the place. There's a spiritual aspect to it."

WOMEN'S WISHES FOR THE FUTURE OF SURFING ARE INEXTRICABLY LINKED TO OUR HOPES FOR FUTURE GENERATIONS AND THE PLANET.

MaKa's inspiration, she said, is Mākaha Beach and the way the Wai'anae community on O'ahu has come together to protect shoreline access and the natural environment there.

"A quality that makes Mākaha unique is that Hawaiian cultural values are still practiced," said forty-five-year resident Kathy Terada. "One of the most important of these is respect—for the ocean, beaches, community, and each other."

In a community centered on surfing, acceptance at Mākaha is earned, she said, by being a good, generous and reliable neighbor both in the lineup and on land.

"I remember Uncle George Downing (the big-wave surfer, beachboy, and close friend of Buffalo Keaulana) told me Mākaha was one of the last places where everybody takes care of each other and each other's children. That really resonated with me," Kathy said. "We all watch the water, watch each others' kids, feed everybody."

Members of the community have worked together for decades to preserve and protect Mākaha Beach, demanding that the city and state relocate Farrington Highway inland, off its sands. Former Mākaha lifeguard Brian Keaulana explained that the road literally bisects the beach, dividing the restrooms and canoe hale from the shore so that children are constantly running back and forth across the road. Moving the road inland, up the valley, was recommended in a 1985 study by the U.S. Army Corps of Engineers after major erosion damage to the highway and beach occurred during high storm waves and flooding streams in1983; the community's concerns have grown more urgent with sea level rise due to climate change. They worry about safety and being cut off from medical care, school, work, grocery stores, and other vital services if the road is washed out.

Surfers have played a leadership role in environmental protection in Hawai'i since waterman John Kelly founded Save Our Surf in the mid-1960s; the group's political activism stopped more than twenty-seven developments that threatened surfing and fishing reefs throughout the islands; it saved an estimated 140 surf sites on O'ahu's South Shore alone. George Downing took the helm at SOS after Kelly's death in 2007. After George died in 2018, his son Keone has carried the mission forward, opposing the proposed addition of massive t-head groins extending over the reef and out into George's beloved Māmala Bay at Waikīkī.

Surfrider Foundation's Hawai'i chapter helped defeat a harbor expansion project to dynamite the reef that would destroy the world-renowned "freight train" wave at Mā'alea, Maui. Surfrider's local chapters team up with other nonprofits, such as Kōkua Hawai'i Foundation, Friends of Kewalos, Sustainable Coastlines, Defend O'ahu Coalition, the University of Hawai'i at Mānoa Marine Biology Laboratory, and Keep the Country Country, to reduce the use and disposal of plastics and their pollution of the sea, organize regular beach cleanups, prevent stormwater runoff from storm drains, sewage and septic systems, conduct regular water bacterial testing at popular surfing beaches, and defend public access to the ocean.

Wai'anae surfers, fishers, and other oceangoers have been working with city, state, and private nonprofit environmental groups to stop dive tours from disturbing resting spinner dolphins, clean beaches and streams, clear invasive plants, and report illegal dumping and waste at beach parks. "I'm hoping generations to come can still seek the joy we have at Mākaha, of being in an ocean that stays clean," Kathy Terada said.

# MĀLAMA 'ĀINA AND KAI

Preserving our waves requires protecting ocean ecosystems.

Here are five ways you can help protect ocean ecosystems.

1. Use reef-friendly sunscreens—they're healthier for you, too. Hawai'i has banned the sale of sunscreens containing some petrochemical active ingredients, but safest are all-mineral sunscreens. See FriendsofHanauma Bay.org and ewg.org/sunscreen/.

2. Keep plastics out of the sea; it entangles and gets ingested by marine life. Choose reusable drink bottles; recycle; pick up trash. Visit Kokuahawaiifoundation.org and Sustainablecoastlineshawaii.org.

3. Help prevent stormwater runoff (silt, fertilizers, sewage, and petrochemicals harm sea life) and prevent erosion with ocean-friendly landscaping. See Surfrider.org.

4. Choose sustainably harvested seafood. See seafoodwatch.org and localiahawaii.com.

5. Buy greener and consume less, including conventional surfboards, which release 375 pounds of $CO_2$ each from manufacture to disposal, concluded a 2009 study at the U.C. Berkeley Energy and Sustainable Technologies Lab. Repair, sell, swap, or donate old surfboards; try models incorporating recycled, more durable, wood and/or plant-based materials. See ecoboard.sustainablesurf.org and hawaiibc.com.

# CHAPTER 10

# TAKING FLIGHT

When I am riding a wave, I feel in the moment and alive. All my senses are engaged. I feel its contours under my feet, hear the hum of my board planing the surface and the crunch and explosion of whitewater, the wind whistling in my ears and the quiet when I'm pitched underwater or, miraculously, rarely, find myself inside the tube, that blue room. On the good rides, I feel relaxed and loose, going with the flow, alternating bursts of straight-ahead speed and cutting back with turns that splash whitewater like accent marks in a musical phrase.

← Pro Surfer Brooke Rudow surfing on a longboard in Waikīkī.

Bit-by-bit, women are claiming more room and opportunities in the waves. "Surfing used to be a male-dominated sport," Sanoe Lake said. "Nowadays, when you hit the lineup you see a change."

THE HAWAIIAN WAY OF SURFING CAN HELP SHAPE THE FUTURE.

– U'ILANI MACABIO

You hear a change, too, among the youngest generation as I did one morning at Suis with weak, tiny waves. There was a flurry of splashing as a group of three eleven-year-old groms tried for a ripple and missed.

"I'm so frustrated!" piped one boy, waving his skinny arms.

The second boy gazed towards the shore. "I thought Leila was coming out with Malia them."

"Leila," the third one said in an awestruck tone. "If Leila was here, she'd be catching everything, even if there's nothing. She surfs circles around me!"

"I hope she doesn't come out," the first one said.

"They're not coming. It's too late," said the second one.

They all cheered at that, but half-heartedly. Then they looked a bit downcast. I could tell they missed the girls and the thrill of watching Leila shred the waves.

Thank goodness, I thought, you can't—yet—bring cell phones out in the waves. The boys had to imagine Leila's surfing, projecting a life-size form on a board in the actual waves, which required active mental exercise rather than passive staring. As for Leila, being talked about gave her a mystical aura and a presence that was arguably more powerful and lasting than that of a miniature figure confined to a screen. And the beauty of it was, she didn't even know she was being talked about—no clicks or likes left behind. She didn't need to know. A real star shouldn't.

As for more opportunities to surf in real life, that requires active effort on our part: The more we speak up and support one another, the more awareness we'll build and convert to chances.

What else do women wish for the future of surfing? "I wish my girls would grow up and be awesome surfers," Kiana Blankenfeld said. "That's the one thing I'm hoping."

"I'm hoping the joy of surfing will continue," Kathy Terada said. "It's getting harder and harder because every place is so crowded. Sometimes there's a lot of negativity out there, or injuries."

But surfers who call Mākaha home, she said, recognize and respect talent and understand surf etiquette, which helps to protect and keep everyone safe, "especially our children."

In summation, Kathy said, "My hope for the future is that we continue to live and honor the core values of Hawaiian culture so the magic of Mākaha continues."

The Hawaiian way of surfing can help shape the future, U'ilani Macabio said, "because the Hawaiians took play seriously. They believed in having fun as well as in hard work, and surfing was a sport that strengthened the entire body."

↑ Collecting autographs at the 2019 Billabong Pipe Masters, Van's Triple Crown of Surfing, Banzai Pipeline on the North Shore of O'ahu.

# Catherine Toth Fox wishes kids in the future

will be able to enjoy surfing for fun, and entering competitions if they want, instead of feeling it's not worth it unless they excel in the eyes of others. She said she worries about the professionalization and commercialization of the sport, which makes young people feel pressured to become not only a competitive surfer but a celebrity.

From one of her North Shore friends, a former pro surfer and now a respected surfing coach, Cat said she's learned that kids in the country have been competing since they were three years old. And it's been that way for more than a decade.

"If you try to start at ten years old, it's too late," Cat said. "You see these kids, age six, seven, or eight, going to the beach with coaches and photographers, because you have to create a social media presence."

# A few summers ago, Suis reached peak grom.

Male tweens and teens were everywhere. Underfoot. Flying in your face. Raining down on you, literally.

All the other surfers were talking about it.

"What's with all the groms? Has there been a hatch somewhere?" asked Mark, a normally mellow musician. shaking his head. "There are, like, fifteen of them and they all paddle for every single wave."

We agreed it would be amusing, like watching spider monkeys doing aerials at the zoo, if only we didn't have to share the cage. There's no escaping the physical bounds of the lineup.

"Please stop paddling in front of me as if I don't exist," I finally told one grom when he paddled back out after riding a wave he had blocked me on. "I exist, you know—I am a human being."

Eyes wide, he turned and made eye contact with me for the first time. "Oh! Sorry," he said. As the mom of a boy, I could tell the apology was sincere, so I introduced myself.

"Hi, Mindy. I'm Dakota," he said with a friendly smile, and from then on, Dakota took care not to paddle in front of me and would always acknowledge my existence with a nod of greeting, although he continued to battle me for waves.

In October, following the summer of peak grom, I paddled out to Suis after work, even though the sun was setting, cold winds were whipping the minuscule waves and it was crowded. Never mind. It was my birthday.

The lineup was filled with sixteen-year-old groms and my heart sank. But I saw Dakota was among them and paddled over.

"It's my birthday, so how about giving me a wave," I said.

His eyes widened. "How old are you?"

I paused. "I am a thousand years old."

He cracked up. "Everybody, next wave is Mindy's, it's her birthday," he told the other groms. Their eyes widened, too, but their faces remained otherwise impassive.

I missed it, of course, but the groms pretended not to see and, to my surprise, they allowed me more chances. I got waves and the conditions didn't seem so bad, after all. Sometimes, even when Dakota had priority in the peak, he'd turn to me and ask politely with just a touch of Hawaiian irony, "Want this one?"

As the sun set and the waves began to melt into the dark, he urged me to start paddling sooner. "Go, Mindy!" he'd shout as a wave loomed outside. "Go! Go-o-o!"

My heart flooded with memories of other nightfalls in the lineup, long ago, the faces of the waves and surfers illuminated by the moon, the sunset or the lighthouse beam, as the boys of the Tongg's Gang shouted at me to go, go, go.

It was the best of birthday gifts, I thought—the thousand-year-old woman restored, briefly, to youth.

Surfing also stimulated the imagination, fostering innovative problem-solving. "Hawaiians were always observing nature, looking and how and why things work, and trying to progress and make things easier in their work; they would ask questions, then they would test it," U'ilani said. "In stories I heard from my kūpuna, if they were traveling by foot around the island and they couldn't get down into a bay, they'd paddle back with a canoe or board and surf in."

Hawaiians were ingenious in sports, she added. "When the waves were junk, they said, 'I'm going to surf the land,' so they invented hōlua," sliding down hills and sand dunes on wooden sleds.

Other times, to reproduce the sensation of flight in surfing on waveless days, the Hawaiians would take to the air. "They would recite their genealogy, jump off massive cliffs, grab the leaves of those huge loulu palms, and trust they would land safely." As a child, U'ilani loved her friend's grandmother's stories of "going on her grandma's back and flying through the valleys."

It's a powerful image for women's surfing—we're taking flight, and we've got each other's backs with new generations carrying forward the momentum of those who came before. Hawaiian culture was and still is non-ageist. The young appreciate the wisdom and knowledge of the elders, the kūpuna, who teach and perpetuate the culture. It is touching to hear young Hawai'i women surfers pay tribute from the winner's dais to the women of earlier generations who've blazed the way.

Kathy Terada remembers when she was young, admiring the lifestyle of an older woman named Mrs. Wong who lived in a house on the beach at Mākaha. "I thought when I grow up, I want to be like Mrs. Wong, and I've turned into Mrs. Wong," she said.

↑ Pro surfer Kristen Magelssen surfing on a longboard in Waikīkī.

Surfing Ala Moana Bowls.

Emily Erickson, an invitee to the 2023 Eddie Aikau
Big Wave contest at Waima Bay, free surfs Waimea in 2020.
Photo by Craig T. Kojima/Honolulu Star-Advertiser

Stephanie Gilmore autographs surfboard for fans.

Jess Shedlock waiting for a wave while surfing in Waikīkī.

# In late July, after a historic big swell

on the South Shore had faded and left a few small rollers behind, I walked up to the Diamond Head Cliffs lookout and passed a boy of ten or so, carrying a shortboard and walking behind his little sister, who was slight and thin and looked about seven years old, carrying her bodyboard and fins. They were shivering, walking barefoot in their wet swimsuits, their faces drained with exhaustion. The girl was frowning; she looked fierce. "You got so many great waves out there," the boy suddenly exclaimed. "Thanks," said the girl, and although she didn't smile (this was serious, she knew she was good), her features relaxed and her eyes shone in the sun's last glow.

Walking back down the hill, I heard someone call my name: It was Dakota, grown up now, watching the sunset with his pretty girlfriend, Vienna. He had graduated from the prestigious California State University Maritime Academy, in Oakland in May, but breaking his arm during a last practice voyage had short-circuited the summer of surfing he'd been looking forward to.

"Look, I got my cast off," he said with an excited smile, holding up his forearm, which was pale and thin and bore a big, ugly scar. He stared eagerly out at Suis. "The doctor said I can't surf yet, but I've been swimming and I nearly took out Vienna's board."

Vienna looked at me and smiled, shaking her head; her elegant shell earrings danced. "No way," she said.

"I'll be seeing you out at Suis pretty soon, Mindy," Dakota said.

"Uh-oh," I said.

"Why? Don't worry, I'm not going to hog all the waves," he said, and Vienna and I laughed. Then I added I looked forward to seeing him back in the lineup soon.

"Women and men are different creatures," Sanoe Lake said. I agree, yet there's another image I can't forget, of a surfer getting barreled in a big Hawaiian wave during a world tour event. All you see is a hand, lower legs and feet; you can't tell whether it's a man or a woman.

As it happens, the photo is from the Maui Women's Pro at Honolua Bay in 2015, and the surfer happens to be one of the many women who got barreled in that event as well as in all the years since at Honolua and Pipeline and all over the world. But it reminds me that surfing, at its best, is a deep, private, gender-neutral communion with a force of nature. In such moments, we are truly free.

↑ Keala Kennelly getting barreled at Pipeline. Photo by Betty Depolito

↓ Justine Dupont, left, and Keala Kennelly surf in the Eddie. → Makani Adric surfs in the Eddie.
Photos by Jamm Aquino/Honolulu Star-Advertiser

# The 2023 Eddie Aikau Big Wave Invitational

Sports history was made on January 22, 2023, when for the first time, women surfed in the storied Eddie Aikau Big-Wave Invitational at Waimea Bay. With offshore winds shaping beautiful but fearsome waves, their steep faces averaging fifty feet high, six women—Hawaiʻi's Makani Adric, Paige Alms, Emily Erickson, Koala Konnelly, and Andrea Moller, and Justine Dupont of France—charged alongside thirty-four men.

North Shore lifeguard Luke Shepardson, twenty-seven, won the event commemorating the late Aikau, the first lifeguard to serve on Oʻahu's North Shore. The joyous celebration of Hawaiian culture also saluted male and female surfers of the past.

"It was beautiful out there," Kennelly said.

THE EDDIE '23

# ENDNOTES

1 Clark, John R.K. *Hawaiian Surfing: Traditions from the Past*. Honolulu: University of Hawai'i Press, 2011.

2 Ibid.

3 Ibid.

4 Ibid.

5 Ibid.

6 Kamakau, Samuel Manaiakalani. *Tales and Traditions of the People of Old*. Honolulu: Bishop Museum Press, 1991.

7 Ibid.

8 Moser, Patrick J. ed. *Pacific Passages: An Anthology of Surf Writing*. Honolulu: University of Hawai'i Press, 2008.

9 Ibid.

10 Ibid.

11 Ibid.

12 Ibid.

13 Westervelt, William D. *Myths and Legends of Hawai'i*. Honolulu: Mutual Publishing, 1897.

14 Ibid.

15 Ibid.

16 Ibid.

17 Ibid.

18 Ibid.

19 Ibid.

20 Clark, John R.K. *Hawaiian Surfing: Traditions from the Past*. Honolulu: University of Hawai'i Press, 2011.

21 Ibid.

22 Ibid.

23 Ibid.

24 Ibid.

25 Ibid.

26 Ibid.

27 Ibid.

28 Brown, Marie Alohalani. *Facing the Spears of Change: The Life and Legacy of John Papa 'Ī'ī*. Honolulu: University of Hawai'i Press, 2016.

# BIBLIOGRAPHY

## BOOKS

Arnell, Carolina. *Surf Like a Girl*. New York, NY: Prestel, 2019.

Beckwith, Martha Warren. *Hawaiian Mythology*. Honolulu: University of Hawai'i Press, 1976.

Brown, Marie Alohalani. *Facing the Spears of Change: The Life and Legacy of John Papa I'i*. Honolulu: University of Hawai'i Press, 2016

Brown, DeSoto. *Surfing*. Honolulu: Bishop Museum Press, 2006.

Clark, John R. K. *Hawai'i Place Names: Shores, Beaches, and Surf Sites*. Honolulu: University of Hawai'i Press, 2002.

Clark, John R. K. *Hawaiian Surfing*. Honolulu: University of Hawai'i Press, 2011.

Clark, Liz. *Swell: A Sailing Surfer's Voyage of Awakening*. California: Patagonia, 2018.

Coleman, Stuart Holmes. *Eddie Would Go*. New York, NY: St. Martin's Press, 2001.

Coleman, Stuart Holmes. *Fierce Heart: The Story of Makaha and the Soul of Hawaiian Surfing*. New York, NY: St. Martin's Press, 2009.

Corte, Ugo. *Dangerous Fun: The Social Lives of Big Wave Surfers*. Chicago: University of Chicago Press, 2022.

Durand, Vicky Heldreich. *Wave Woman*. Phoenix, AZ: SparkPress, 2020.

Einzig, Laura. *Women Making Waves*. NY: Ten Speed Press, 2022.

Finnegan, William. *Barbarian Days: A Surfing Life*. New York: Penguin, 2015.

Hough-Snee, Dexter Zavalza and Alexander Sotelo Eastman, editors. *The Critical Surf Studies Reader*. Durham, NC: Duke University Press, 2017.

Iaukea, Sydney Lehua. *The Queen and I: A Story of Dispossessions*. Berkeley, CA: University of California Press, 2011.

I'i, John Papa. *Fragments of Hawaiian History*. Honolulu: Bishop Museum Press, 1993.

Ingersoll, Karin Amimoto. *Waves of Knowing: A Seascape Epistomology*. Durham, NC: Duke University Press, 2016.

Kamakau, Samuel Manaiakalani. *Tales and Traditions of the People of Old*. Honolulu: Bishop Museum Press, 1991.

Kempton, Jim. *Women on Waves: A Cultural History of Surfing from Ancient Goddesses and Hawaiian Queens to Malibu, Movie Stars and Millennial Champions.* New York, NY: Pegasus Books, 2021.

Lae, Sanoe with Steven Jarrett. *Surfer Girl: A Guide to the Surfing Life.* New York, NY: Little, Brown & Co., 2005.

Lemarie, Jeremy. *Surf: Une Histoire de la Glisse, de la Premiere Vague aux Beach Boys.* Paris, France: Editions Arkhe, 2018.

Lopez, Gerry. *Surf is Where You Find It: The Wisdom of the Waves, Any Time, Anywhere, Any Way.* Ventura, CA: Patagonia Books, 2022.

Moser, Patrick, editor. *Pacific Passages: An Anthology of Surf Writing.* Honolulu: University of Hawai'i Press, 2008.

Nicholson, Joy. *Tribes of Palos Verdes.* NY: Viking Press, 1998.

Pukui, Mary Kawena, Samuel H. Elbert & Esther T. Mookini, editors. *Place Names of Hawaii,* Honolulu: University of Hawai'i Press, 1974.

Walker, Isaiah-Helekunihi. *Waves of Resistance: Surfing and History in Twentieth-Century Hawai'i.* Honolulu: University of Hawai'i Press, 2011.

Warshaw, Matt and William Finnegan, *The Encyclopedia of Surfing,* NY: Houghtin Mifflin Harcourt, 2003.

Westervelt, William C. *Myths and Legends of Hawai'i.* Honolulu: Mutual Publishing, 1997.

## MAGAZINES & PERIODICALS

Duane, Daniel. "The Fight for Gender Equality in one of the most Dangerous Sports on Earth," *The New York Times Magazine,* Feb.7, 2019.

McDougall, Maya. "Black Girls Surf," *Hawaii Business Magazine,* 2020.

Minsberg, Talia. "Finding Gender Equity in the World's Most Famous Waves," *The New York Times,* December 22, 2022.

Orlean, Susan. "Life's Swell," *Outside Magazine,* August 2002.

Pennybacker, Mindy. "In the Lineup," ocean-lifestyles features column, Honolulu Star-Advertiser, 2017-2019; surf sports column, 2021-ongoing.

Pennybacker, Mindy. "Views from Kaimuki: Joey Hamasaki's pan-Pacific path from Town and back again," *The Surfer's Journal,* Vol. 30.4, August/September 2021.

Pennybacker, Mindy. "Women join men in the lineup for historic 'Eddie' surf contest," *Honolulu Star-Advertiser*, Jan. 22, 2023.

Riley-Adams, Ella. "The Ocean Women of Oahu," *Vogue*, March 6, 2019.

Shannon, Marie Quirk, "Kaikaina Surf Girls: The next generation of empowered wahine," Freesurf Magazine, 2021.

Schaffer, Sharon. "Making Waves," op-ed on black women surfers, *The New York Times*, June 4, 2021.

Wallace, Don. "Carissa's World: How a Self-Effacing Girl from Kaimuki Surfed Her Way to Olympic Gold," *Honolulu*, Dec. 2021.

Wallace, Don. "Leading Wahine: These 5 Local Surfers are Blue Crushing It," *Honolulu*, June 2022.


## ONLINE SOURCES

@BanzaiBetty
Accesssurf.org (water programs for people with disabilities)
Beachgrit.com
Blackgirlssurf.org
Browngirlsurf.com
Eos.com (The Encyclopedia of Surfing)
Freesurfmagazine.com
Hasasurf.org (Hawaii Surfing Association)
Historyofwomensurfing.com
Magicseaweed.com
Moorealoha.com (Foundation benefitting girl surfers)
Reiner, Keani, "Hokule'a 1976." youtube.com
Stabmagazine.com
Staradvertiser.com
Surfequity.org (Committee for Equity in Women's Surfing)
Surfer.com (Surfer Magazine)
Surfergirlmag.com
Surfersjournal.com
Surfertoday.com
Surfline.com
Surfnewsnetwork.com
Theinertia.com
Wahinekai.org (Wahine Kai Women's Surf Club)

# ABOUT THE COVER

Sometimes on a crowded day, when everyone's paddling desperately for the same wave, someone will call out, "Party wave!" to break up the tension and urge everyone to ride it together. Usually spontaneous, a party wave is not so easy to plan ahead. Photographer Yoshi Tanaka discovered that in the summer of 2020 when world champion longboarder, Kelia Moniz, pregnant with her first child, asked him to shoot one. She and some girlfriends were going surfing at Canoes in Waikīkī to celebrate one of their birthdays and wanted him to capture them—and no one else—riding a party wave.

"We met by the Duke Kahanamoku statue. They paddled out from there, and then I stood by the lifeguard tower flying the drone," Yoshi said, noting that while he usually shoots surfing from the water, that wouldn't be possible for such a wide-angle shot.

"There were so many of them, it had to be teamwork, everything planned perfect-ly," from getting a wave to themselves in the Waikīkī crowd ("that part, it helped that there were so many of them"), to every surfer keeping their relative position and planned direction as they rode.

"They worked hard, did a couple attempts, some of them failed, and then luckily I got that one image."

Sharing a perfect Waikīkī roller, from left to right, are Malia Mizuno, Keani Canullo, Kelis Kaleopa'a, Tiara Bella Hernandez, Megan Godinez, Kelia Moniz, Nanea Al-den, and Dixie Rose. The photo is currently displayed in the lobby of the Kaimana Beach Hotel in Waikīkī.

# PHOTO CREDITS

p. 47: Keolafirsov | Dreamstime.com

p. 48: Dennis Oda

p. 50: Dennis Oda; background, Epicstock | Dreamstime.com

p. 51: Dennis Oda

p. 52: Mikhail Dudarev | Dreamstime.com

p. 54: Nikki Gensert | Dreamstime.com

p. 55: Kazunori Sano | Dreamstime.com

p. 56: Hawai'i State Archives; background, Jarvis Gray | Dreamstime.com

p. 57: Marcelo Diaz Rodriguez

p. 58: Dennis Oda, *Honolulu Star-Bulletin*

p. 59: John Titchen, *Honolulu Star-Bulletin*

p. 60: top left, Dennis Oda, *Honolulu Star-Bulletin*; center left, Rico Leffanta | Dreamstime.com; bottom left, Bakutis family; all photos on right, Rico Leffanta | Dreamstime.com; background, Keolafirsov | Dreamstime.com

p. 63: both photos courtesy Bakutis family

p. 65: courtesy Kathy Terada

p. 67: Omri Tuab | Dreamstime.com

p. 68: Dennis Oda

p. 70: Cindy Ellen Russell, *Honolulu Star-Advertiser*

p. 73: top left, Jane Gillespie; top right, Rico Leffanta | Dreamstime.com; bottom, Dennis Oda

p. 74: Craig T. Kojima, *Honolulu Star-Advertiser*

p. 76: courtesy Shea Reiner

p. 77: Dennis Oda

p. 78: Maksym Fesenko | Dreamstime.com

p. 80: Darren Baker | Dreamstime.com

p. 82–85: Dennis Oda

p. 86: Dave Miyamoto

p. 87-88: Davidzean | Dreamstime.com

p. 90: River Eaton

p. 91: Universal Studios

p. 92: Scott Winer

p. 93: Dennis Oda

p. 94: Dennis Oda

p. 97: all photos Dennis Oda

p. 98: top, courtesy Kathy Terada; center, Don King; bottom, Ha'a Keaulana

p. 99: both photos Ha'a Keaulana

p. 100: Ha'a Keaulana

p. 101: Ken Sakamoto, *Honolulu Star-Bulletin*

p. 103: top, *Honolulu Star-Bulletin*; center and bottom, Betty Depolito

p. 106: LeRoy Grannis; background, Kia'i Tallett

p. 108: courtesy Evie Black

p. 110: Dennis Oda; background, Keolafirsov | Dreamstime.com

p. 111: Paul Topp | Dreamstime.com

p. 113: Tony Heff

p. 114: Jeff Divine

p. 115: Paul Topp | Dreamstime.com

p. 116: Richard Hallman, courtesy of Keala Kennelly

p. 117: Craig T. Kojima, *Honolulu Star-Advertiser*

p. 119: Paul Topp | Dreamstime.com

p. 122: Dennis Oda

p. 124: Craig T. Kojima, *Honolulu Star-Advertiser*

p. 126: both photos Craig T. Kojima, *Honolulu Star-Advertiser*

p. 128: all photos Paul Topp | Dreamstime.com

The surfer who got snaked at Tongg's (p. 122-23) enjoys a wave all to herself. Photo by Dennis Oda

p. 130: top, Craig T. Kojima, *Honolulu Star-Advertiser;* bottom, Jamm Aquino, *Honolulu Star-Advertiser*

p. 131: Dennis Oda

p. 132: Pavol Stredansky | Dreamstime.com

p. 133: Cindy Ellen Russell, *Honolulu Star-Advertiser*

p. 134: Mindy Pennybacker

p. 136: Dennis Oda

p. 139: top left, Paul Teruya; top right and bottom, Rico Leffanta | Dreamstime.com

p. 140: Danielschreurs | Dreamstime.com

p. 141: Mei-Li Restani, Surfing Moms

p. 142-143: KC Lostetter Photography, Surfing Moms

p. 144-145: Mei-Li Restani, Surfing Moms

p. 146: Mikalai Bachkou | Dreamstime.com

p. 150: courtesy Kiana Blankenfeld

p. 151: Sean Davey

p. 153: Dennis Oda

p. 154: Christa Funk

p. 156-157: Eq Roy | Dreamstime.com

p. 158-159: Paulacobleigh | Dreamstime.com

p. 160: Mike Varney

p. 163: Mark Van Dam | Dreamstime.com

p. 164: top, Kia'i Tallett; bottom, Sachi Cunningham

p. 168: Paul Topp | Dreamstime.com

p. 171: Rico Leffanta | Dreamstime.com

p. 172-173: Glennel Warren | Dreamstime.com

p. 174: Paul Topp | Dreamstime.com

p. 175: top left, Mikalai Bachkou | Dream-

stime.com; top right, Kazunori Sano | Dreamstime.com; center left, Craig T. Kojima, *Honlulu Star-Advertiser;* center right, Rico Leffanta | Dreamstime.com; bottom, Paul Topp | Dreamstime.com

p. 176: Denis Moskvinov | Dreamstime.com

p. 177: Betty Depolito

p. 178-179: Jamm Aquino, *Honolulu Star-Advertiser*

p. 180 Tropicdreams | Dreamstime.com

p. 187: Dennis Oda

p. 188: Bruce Asato, *Honolulu Star-Advertiser*

p. 190: E.Y.Y. Yanagi

# ACKNOWLEDGMENTS

As a surfing writer, I am indebted to the Hawaiian people, who brought he'e nalu into the world; and the wave-riding wahine whose stories bring this book to life: Laola Lake Aea, Ane Bakutis, Helena Bakutis-Kekaula, Rochelle Ballard, Evie Black, Kiana Blankenfeld, Mikayla Brennan, Mahina Chillingworth, Isabel Cleofe, Betty Depolito, Kai'ulu Downing, Sanoe Lake Eaton, Vicky Heldreich Durand, Catherine Toth Fox, Kim Heyer, Sydney Iaukea, Karin Amimoto Ingersoll, Heather Nahaku Kalei, May Kamaka, Keala Kennelly, Melissa Kurpinski, Sally Lundburg, U'ilani Macabio, Elizabeth Madin, Cappy Makaiau, Jyoti Mau, Debbie Millikan, Cristal Mortensen, Andree Paradis, Wendy Sakuma, Kathy Terada, and Jennifer Lee Van Gieson.

Indispensable ideas and guidance came from brilliant editor and page designer Jane Gillespie and sage publisher Bennett Hymer at Mutual Publishing; my invincible agent Jeff Kleinman; and my assiduous in-house editors Don, Rory, and Kaitlin Wallace.

The stellar photos were shot expressly for the book by Dennis Oda and Eric Yanagi, or included with permission from the *Honolulu Star-Advertiser* and independent photographers Sachi Cunningham, Sean Davey, Jeff Divine, Christa Funk, LeRoy Grannis, Richard Hallman, Tony Heff, Ha'a Keaulana, Don King, Gary Knights, Dave Miyamoto, Marcelo Diaz Rodriguez, Kia'i Tallett, Yoshi Tanaka, Paul Teruya, Mike Varney and Scott Winer. My heartfelt thanks to you for illuminating and elevating this text.

Homage is due to *Star-Advertiser's* masterful photographers George Lee, Craig T. Kojima, Cindy Ellen Russell, Bruce Asato and Jamm Aquino, all such a joy to work with; and editors Curtis Murayama and Christie Wilson, who've nurtured my surf articles, a few brief selections from which appear in altered form herein.

In and out of the lineup, consistent support has flowed from the Pennybacker-Wallace-Kolivas-Won ohana; hanai sisters Dee Jay and Franny; Tongg's alums Donny, Alika, Brian, Warren and Dale; and Suis mensches Kimo, Kawika, Chris, Russell, John, Paul, Dakota, Will, Marc, Stuart, Mark, Peter, Tanner, Ben, Jimmy, Gerald and Jeff.

Mahalo and aloha to everyone.

← *Carissa Moore free surfs at her home break, Kewalo Basin, in Honolulu. Photo by Bruce Asato/ Honolulu Star-Advertiser*

# ABOUT THE AUTHOR

Photo © 2022 by E.Y.Y. Yanagi

Honolulu native Mindy Pennybacker is a surf columnist for the *Honolulu Star-Advertiser* and former editor-in-chief of *Honolulu Weekly* and *The Green Guide*, an award-winning, national environmental newsletter.

The author of *Do One Green Thing* (Harper-Collins, 2010), her writing has appeared in *The Atlantic, Surfers' Journal, The Nation, The New York Times, Bamboo Ridge, Glamour, Martha Stewart's Whole Living*, and *The Village Voice*. Her fiction writing has received a National Endowment for the Arts Fellowship and Wallace Stegner, Joseph Henry Jackson, and James Michener Awards.

A graduate of Punahou School, Stanford University, the University of Iowa Writers Workshop, and the University of California at Davis, Martin Luther King School of Law, Mindy learned community engagement from her grandparents, Lawrence and Mary Kang, who owned and produced Halm's Kim Chee for more than thirty years; and her mother Dolly Kang Lott, who taught piano, founded Rainbow Peace Fund, and served on the State of Hawai'i Martin Luther King, Jr. Commission.

Mindy lives on O'ahu and Belle Ile en Mer, France, with her husband Don Wallace, author of *The French House* (Sourcebooks, 2014), contributing editor at *Honolulu Magazine* and co-founder of *The Hawaii Review of Books*. In their free time they enjoy riding waves and consuming local foods on both islands with Rory and Kaitlin Wallace.